Rapid Ray

The Story of Ray Lewis

JOHN COOPER

Tundra Books

Published in Canada by Tundra Books,
481 University Avenue, Toronto, Ontario M5G 2E9

Published in the United States by Tundra Books of Northern New York,
P.O. Box 1030, Plattsburgh, New York 12901

Library of Congress Control Number: 2002101148

National Library of Canada Cataloguing in Publication Data

Cooper, John, 1958-
Rapid Ray : the story of Ray Lewis

Includes index.
ISBN 0-88776-612-9

1. Lewis, Ray, 1910- 2. Runners (Sports) – Canada – Biography.
3. Pullman porters – Canada – Biography. 4. Black Canadians –
Biography. I. Title.

GV1061.15.L49C659 2002   796.42'092   C2002-900781-X

We acknowledge the support of the Canada Council for the Arts and the
Ontario Arts Council for our publishing program.

We acknowledge the financial support of the Government of Canada
through the Book Publishing Industry Development Program for our
publishing activities.

We acknowledge that all photographs are used with permission.

Design: Blaine Herrmann

Printed and bound in Canada

1 2 3 4 5 6   07 06 05 04 03 02

*I dedicate my life story to young Canadians who,
every day, are working hard to achieve their goals,
as athletes and individuals.*

– Ray Lewis

*Dedicated to my wife, Maria, with my gratitude
for her love and commitment.*

– John Cooper

ACKNOWLEDGEMENTS

The author wishes to acknowledge and thank the
following people for their support and encouragement:
Beverly Bowen, Lawrence Hill, and Ken Pearson.
My sincere thanks also to publisher Kathy Lowinger
of Tundra Books and to editor Kat Mototsune.

TABLE OF CONTENTS

AUTHOR'S NOTES

On Measurements

Ray Lewis ran in many different races during his career. While we generally use the metric system today, in Ray's time as a runner, races in North America and Britain were measured in imperial measure (using the yard or the mile as a measurement) and European races were measured in the metric system (using meters).

In the imperial system, there are twelve inches in a foot, and three feet in a yard. One mile is 1760 yards, or 5280 feet. To convert the imperial measurement to metric terms, use the following table:

> One mile = 1.6093 kilometers
> One yard = 0.9144 meters
> One foot = 0.3048 meters
> One inch = 2.54 centimeters

On the Narration

I have told this story in the voice of Ray Lewis. Aside from the many hours spent writing the text, this book represents well over 100 hours of personal interviews with Ray Lewis, both in person and over the telephone, as well as additional research in libraries, museums, and churches, and with experts in African-Canadian history. It is written in Ray's voice, as the experiences detailed within it are Ray's; I have made no attempt to create a separate author's voice or to speak for another culture. This is Ray's story of his life and experiences, and the author expresses the sincerest of thanks to Ray for his cooperation, his kindness, and his wonderful sense of magnanimity and brotherhood in bringing his story to a new audience. He is truly a great man whose achievements deserve to be recognized and applauded by future generations.

CHAPTER 1

MY EARLY YEARS

◆

*My name is Raymond Gray Lewis. Most people just
call me Ray. But there was a time when just about the
only name I was known by was Rapid Ray, in my
hometown of Hamilton, Ontario, and across Canada.*

Why was I called Rapid Ray? Because I could outrun just
about any other opponent when I was young.

Of course, I was called a lot of other names too, mostly
because of my skin color. Being a Canadian of African
descent, I grew up during a time, in the early part of the
20th century, when being black meant that you were
treated differently than people with light skin. It was a
time of terrible discrimination. You had to struggle. You
might have to fight hard for a job. You could expect to be
turned down for a loan from a bank if you were trying to
buy a house. In school, you were likely to be teased or
called names by your classmates – and the white teachers
might treat you poorly – all because of the color of your
skin. Even just buying a loaf of bread at the grocery store,
getting a table in a restaurant, or trying to sit in the front
section of a movie theater could be difficult. Black people

in Canada and the United States, the descendants of
slaves brought to work on farms and plantations, had
to fight for respect every day of their lives. As the great-
grandson of former slaves, it was no different for me.

I had to put up with all kinds of name calling, by
other kids and later by adults, whether I was running to
school, racing around the block, or competing in track-
and-field meets across the country. But you can believe
me when I tell you that being treated poorly by others
didn't defeat me. It only made me want to run harder, to
prove to everyone that I could achieve great things.

I ran so hard, in fact, that I went all the way to the
Olympic Games in Los Angeles, California, and to
the British Empire Games in London, England, where
I even sat down to dinner with royalty.

While I was training as an athlete for the Olympics, I
worked hard, too, as a railway porter on the Canadian
Pacific Railway, serving people who were traveling across
Canada and into the United States.

I was born in Hamilton, on Clyde Street, on
October 8, 1910. Hamilton is known as Canada's Steel
Town, and it produces much of the steel used in manufacturing things we use every day, from cars and stoves to
refrigerators, tools, and machinery. It was – and still is –
a very busy city. I grew up watching cargo carriers steam
into the harbor with raw iron ore; people bustled about
the streets to and from work, and horses pulled wagons
that carried milk, eggs, and bread to customers throughout the city.

I was the youngest child of Cornelius and Emma
Lewis. My eldest brother was Victor, followed by my
sister Marjorie, then my brother Howard, and finally me.
My parents taught me the value of working hard. That
meant working hard in school and, when I became an
athlete, training hard too.

I attended Wentworth Street Public School. I used
to get up in the morning, have my breakfast, and, while I
didn't dawdle too much, sometimes I had to run hard to
get to school before the bell at nine o'clock a.m. Lucky
for me, the school was only about a block and a half away.
I'm pleased to say that I was never late to school, not even
one day, even though I had to run hard to get there at
times. It was a big public school for the time – two storeys
high, with several hundred students and more than twelve
rooms. Many years after I attended it, Wentworth Public
School was closed and later torn down to make way for an
apartment building.

Growing up on Clyde Street was fun. The younger I
was, the less fuss white people made about the color of my
skin. My friends and I used to play hockey on the streets
and, where buses, cars, and trucks now drive through
Hamilton's busy downtown core, the milkman and the
bread man would come down the street in their wagons,
pulled by big, strong horses, clip-clopping along at a slow
but steady pace. On Friday nights, the farmers would
come up nearby Cannon Street, their horse-drawn wagons
loaded with produce, heading for the market that opened
on Saturday morning. In those days before refrigerators,

the ice wagon was another sight, trundling down the street, delivering huge blocks of ice. The iceman was big, with broad shoulders and thick, ropy arms. He'd use long iron tongs to grab a block of ice, then sling it over his shoulder to make his delivery, whistling as he headed into one of many houses that had an icebox.

Once in a while, kids would swipe a peach or other piece of fruit from a passing farmer's wagon. Police officers, patrolling the downtown neighborhood on bicycles, would chase the rascals through the streets, but the kids usually got away. While some people owned automobiles, they were expensive and were rare sights. Most people got around by walking or on bicycles, or they used the streetcar.

When I was growing up, streetcars were a familiar sight along what was called the Belt Line, which ran through Hamilton's downtown core. And just two blocks from my house was the car barn where streetcars were repaired. My friends and I would watch the streetcars being moved around in the big yard where they were stored. We would watch and marvel at the mechanics working on the big streetcar engines.

Just down the street from my house was the fire hall. My friends and I might be playing in Woodland Park, not far from my home, and hear the siren of the fire wagon as the firefighters took off, slapping the reins of their horses in response to a call. That was a call to us too. We dropped our gloves and bats and took off towards the station. We would run alongside the horses as they charged out of the firehouse. We could run as fast as the hook-and-ladder wagon for about 50 or 60 metres, even taking off ahead of them for a while. I would always be out in front of my friends, almost nose to nose with a big bay mare, hearing the huffing of her breath as the firefighters urged her on. I would listen to the sound of the horses' hooves pounding on the street before they would pick up their pace and canter off ahead of us up the street, leaving us to catch our breath in the dust they stirred up.

I ran everywhere. I would run past the train station and see the passengers boarding or disembarking, and the porters, all of them black like me, stooping to pick up bags or to help people onto the train – always smiling, always polite.

During the week, I would have to run over to Barton Street to get coal oil for our family's lamps. Like a car, electricity was an expensive commodity, and it would be a few years before we could afford to have electricity put into our house.

For kids, watching sports, as well as playing them, was a great way to have fun, and Hamilton in those days was home to many great sports teams, like the Hamilton Tigers of the NHL. The Hamilton Tigers hockey team would play against Ottawa, Toronto, and Montreal at the Hamilton Arena, which was owned by the Abso-Pure (for "absolutely pure") Ice Company, at the corner of Wentworth and Barton Streets. Not only did the company sell ice – it had the best ice surface in the city!

Thanks to Canadian athletes like Ned Hanlan, rowing was a popular sport in the early 20th century, but it was soon replaced by competitive bicycling. Soccer was also played, largely between teams from the different companies in the city. There was the Hamilton Tigers football team, which had been around since 1869 and which later became the Hamilton Tiger-Cats of the Canadian Football League. Hamilton was also known as a great track-and-field city, with many leading athletes coming to town for meets. We had our own track-and-field heroes and champions, like Billy Sherring, who won the marathon at the Athens Olympic Games in 1906, and Bobby Kerr, winner of the 220-meter race at the 1908 Olympic Games, who later managed the Olympic track-and-field team.

At Woodland Park, there was a softball diamond, and its green spaces were a gathering place for many people, who would get together to listen to band concerts on Friday nights, a big social event in the community.

As I said, adults walked, bicycled, or took the streetcar. But kids ran everywhere. It was a community where neighborhoods were tightly knit and people knew each other. It was easy to run from one place to another, dodging the occasional ice wagon or jumping out of the way of a bicycle when you heard the familiar *ring-ring* of its bell. Everywhere I went children ran through the streets.

For entertainment, I often went to the Savoy Theatre with friends to see the movies. The price of admission

was 35 cents for the floor seats and 25 cents for the loges
seating upstairs. Most people would pay the extra dime
to sit on the lower level, because it gave you a better
view of the movie. I would have my money ready at the
ticket window. But I always would be sold a 25-cent
ticket, no questions asked, on the assumption that
because I was black I could not afford a 35-cent ticket.
I would have to insist on buying the 35-cent ticket. It
was something that I got used to, and going to the movies
gave me a chance to develop a love for good entertainment. Much later, when I worked as a railway porter,
that love would carry me through many years of lonely
stops in big cities across Canada.

When I was in my teens, I even had a chance to work
for a theater owner named Mr. Guest who ran two movie
theaters, the Empire Theatre and the Queen's Theatre.
My job was to carry reels of film back and forth between
the two theaters. The movies were mostly cowboy pictures
or action movies. Mr. Guest would pay my way to and
from each theater on the jitney, a small bus that ran a
regular route around Hamilton. I was paid 10 cents per
reel of film; one day I made 70 cents when the theater
showed the big picture *The Four Horsemen of the
Apocalypse*. And that was a lot of money at the time.

When I was a child, life had enough funny events to
make it interesting. For instance, around that time, my
friends and I were in the habit of teasing an elderly couple
that lived behind Wentworth Street School. We would

knock on their door and run away, laughing when the old woman would come to the door, look out, and find no one there.

On one particular day we had knocked on the door and ran off as usual. But on the street next to mine, one of my friends yelled to me, "She's following you!" Sure enough the old lady was hot on my heels. I got home and a little girl from across the street called out to the old woman, "He lives in there!" and pointed to our house. This is before we had a porch; there were some concrete blocks that served as steps up to the front door. I had already scrambled up the steps and shot into the house, while the old woman stormed across the street. Soon she was rapping hard at our door.

I was quaking as my sister Marjorie answered the door. I was certain that I was going to be in big trouble, and my parents always wanted to avoid trouble with the neighbors. Now, Marjorie had medium-brown skin and I'm a little lighter. The woman saw Marjorie and said, "Oh, I'm sorry, I've got the wrong house." She must have thought, from a distance, that I was white and so couldn't have lived there. Confused, she turned and went home. We had a good laugh over that; and it has happened to me at other times in my life as well. My light complexion sometimes fooled people, from a distance, into thinking that I was white.

I did a lot of my growing up during World War I. The war began in 1914, and ended on November 11, 1918. At the time, Canada had a population of seven million; under Prime Minister Sir Robert Borden, able-bodied men were urged to join the fight. Around 620,000 men joined the Canadian Army and a total of 59,544 Canadians lost their lives in the war.

For kids, it was an exciting time. "Let's go!" my friends would yell, and we would run up Cannon Street to see the trucks and the soldiers on their way to the James Street Armouries. We would watch the military trucks thunder past, raising little dust devils in the early sun, their gears grinding, engines huff-puffing. Up close, we could feel the rumble of their engines in our bones; the sound of that heavy equipment shifting gears carried through the neighborhood. It added to the general stir of excitement that became a part of day-to-day life: Canada's war effort was important, and even as a youngster, I could feel it stir something inside of me as much as the rumble of the trucks going by was felt in my bones.

The scene was always enthusiastic, with people on the street cheering and waving to the soldiers. No one thought about death at the hands of the Germans thousands of miles away – everybody thought only of fighting for our country and for Great Britain. We followed the trucks up every street and it was a thrill for us to see the soldiers in their crisp new uniforms, tilting their heads slightly at us as they went past in military precision. Soldiers smiled at the crowds, one arm swinging, the other holding a rifle.

Enlistment officials would stop men on the street, putting a hand on an arm and urging them to listen. They

called out to the crowds in loud, strained voices. "Come
with us to fight the Germans! Come on! Come with us!"
they would shout. "Fight for democracy. Fight for
freedom." It was a common sight to see men in business
suits, or workmen in coveralls, or young men barely out
of their teens – each and every one stirred by patriotism
and a desire to fight for freedom – asking for information
on signing up.

It wasn't long before we heard warplanes, something
new to us, buzzing overhead. In fact, the airplane had
only been around for eleven years before the war started;
it was so new and different that the sound of one passing
overhead was guaranteed to stop people in their tracks.
They would look up, cheer, and wave to the pilot.

At Gore Park, a public square and important gathering
place in Hamilton's downtown, rallies were held to aid in
the war effort and to keep everybody's patriotic feelings
high. There were demonstrations of modern tanks,
looking to us like blocks of solid steel as they pivoted
on tractor treads, their gun turrets swiveling, crushing
railway boxcars to show just how powerful they were.
It was an impressive sight. During the demonstrations,
people were urged to buy Victory Bonds to help raise
money for the war effort.

It wasn't always easy for the black community, though.
While some African-Canadians were accepted into the
service early on, too often black men were turned away.
This happened in many communities across Canada,
including Hamilton.

I would hear of black men being told by recruiters "We can't use you!" even though the country desperately needed soldiers. A few African-Canadians fought in the war in all-black, segregated units, and there were others whose service was confined mainly to military construction crews. But the black community still felt a wave of patriotism as strong as that felt in the white community. We wanted to do our part for the war effort.

It would be more than four hard years of fighting before the war ended. But when a bit of good news got out, people would overreact – they were all too happy and eager to hear that the fighting was ended. A few days before World War I was officially over, a false announcement rippled through our neighborhood. We all thought the war was over; the man who lived next door ran into his backyard and began tooting his bugle. Turns out he was getting a head start on celebrations, but it wasn't long before the real victory was finally announced. The following year, 1919, there were Victory Bond parades. People sang, they held parties, and they danced down the streets, arm in arm. I recall my father on one of the floats sponsored by the company he worked for as a janitor; he was standing tall and proud, smiling and waving to the crowd.

In the winter of 1918–1919, the great influenza epidemic hit Hamilton in the same way it hit other cities across North America and around the world – with pain and misery. Some experts said it killed 20 million people worldwide; others said it might have killed even more, up to 50 million. There were cities whose funeral parlors didn't have enough coffins to handle all the deaths. In Hamilton, more than 5000 people died. In our own house, my sister Marjorie and brother Victor became very ill and lay close to death for many days. We did not expect them to survive.

I would walk slowly from Marjorie's room to Victor's room, speaking to my mother in whispers, watching my sister and brother shiver and shake in the light from the coal oil lamps. Their eyes were tired and their teeth chattered. At my young age, I didn't understand death and didn't really know what to expect. However, given that the epidemic would go on to kill hundreds in our city, I was sadly waiting for their end to come. Doctors were pressed into service and our own family doctor found it hard to pay a visit, since there were many more who were also sick and in need of help. But Marjorie and Victor lived. Eventually they got stronger until they both made complete recoveries.

Those were difficult times for many people. The war took away many husbands, fathers, and brothers. And the flu took away even more family members across the city. As well, the economy was poor.

During times of high unemployment, many people, especially men, rode in boxcars from one city to the next as hobos, looking for work. Later on, these men would become the subject of songs, stories and movies, with their lives portrayed as carefree and happy. There would be stories telling of them seated around a fire in an open field, cooking a can of pork and beans and heating up a pot of coffee, singing happy songs. The reality was that they desperately needed work.

When I was young and my father was at his job, hobos would sometimes knock at the back door. A hobo would be standing on the stoop, holding his battered hat in his hands, his face earnest. He would ask, politely as possible, if there was any work that needed to be done around the house. Hobos were well known for never taking a handout. They always wanted to earn their money. If there was an odd job around the house, my mother would ask the hobo to do it – rake leaves, clean up the yard, move furniture. As long as the children were in the house, she would invite him in for a sandwich afterwards. I always had a genuine feeling that the hobos and other unemployed people wanted to work hard for money and a meal. And though their clothes might be worn, they were generally clean and the men carried themselves with dignity.

A big part of the black community was the church. Like it or not, we kids either went happily, or we were cajoled, dragged, or pushed into attending church every Sunday morning.

In Hamilton's black community, St. Paul's African Methodist Episcopal Church was an important part, not only of the family, but also of African-Canadian social life. It was the home of the longest surviving black

congregation in Hamilton, founded in 1835 in a log
structure on Rebecca Street. (It later moved to a wooden
building in 1879, which was remodelled as a brick building
in 1905.)

The African Methodist Episcopal, or AME, Church
was founded by Richard Allen. Allen was a former slave
who preached the Christian gospel of Methodism in
the early years of the 19th century. In Philadelphia he
formed the AME Church and drew many people from the
surrounding communities. The AME Church arrived in
Canada in the 1830s. After the Civil War ended in 1865,
some Canadian AME Churches changed their names to
British Methodist Episcopal, or BME, Church to show
allegiance to Queen Victoria of England.

St. Paul's became a vital part of the lives of blacks of
Hamilton who had entered Canada to escape slavery in
the United States. It later became a non-denominational
church and its name was changed to Stewart Memorial
Church. For Hamilton's black community, which was
small and spread throughout the city, church activities
provided an opportunity to get to know one another in
a place where we wouldn't feel the sting of the white
community's racism. Across the city, you might find the
occasional black family at one of the Catholic churches
or at one of the other denominations, such as the Baptist
church. But most of them were associated with either
AME or BME churches.

My parents were regular churchgoers and took us to
church every week. I was christened at St. Paul's, and as a

young child I sat with my family in the church's northeast corner pews. St. Paul's became an important part of my life. I was the secretary of the Sunday school at age twelve, and I still serve on my church's Board of Trustees.

Every week we walked up Cannon Street, then down to the church on John Street. I can remember my father pushing me in a little homemade go-cart to church. I especially liked going over the rippled part of the sidewalk, which was built so that horses making deliveries wouldn't slip on the concrete.

We patiently listened to the minister's sermon and, in Sunday school, learned the lessons we needed to learn, not only about religion, but to help us deal with a world outside that treated us differently because of our skin color. After Sunday school we would ride on the Belt Line streetcar, which for 3 cents would take us around the city. There was also the radial car – a big, fast, streetcar-like vehicle – which would take us to Beamsville or Oakville. And in the harbor was moored the White Star, a sidewheel steamship that took people to the Canadian National Exhibition in Toronto. Overall, the pace of life on a Sunday was relaxed. People weren't in a hurry and they took the time to enjoy life.

On Sunday afternoon we had an early supper. It was a special day and the dinner was a special one, usually roast chicken or beef, potatoes, and other vegetables. There was never any liquor in our house. For my father and mother, who worked hard every day, Sunday really was a day of rest. On Sunday evening the family would

get down on our knees and pray together, with my father
leading the prayers.

We would sometimes have Tom Thumb weddings at
the church, where young children would dress up in their
parents' clothes and recite their lines. We had concerts
and recitations. You could make your own music if you
had a choir or a band. In the evening, a phonograph, an
early version of the record player, would play music. It
was plain and wholesome entertainment.

For Hamilton's black community, a variety of church
events served a vital function in keeping us in touch
with each other. There was an annual picnic in nearby
Grimsby, attracting hundreds of African-Canadians
who would come by boat from Toronto or via radial
cars. The picnic later became a larger event and moved
to Port Dalhousie.

While St. Paul's community was predominantly black,
I recall one or two white families who were happily
accepted by the congregation. I emphasize "happily"
because it wasn't the same way around for black families
who tried to join white churches. They were too often
rejected. Black families that were new to the city might
attend services at a predominantly white church and
would later be drawn aside by the minister and be told
"there is a nice church over on John Street where you will
find some friends." In other words, the message was that
they were clearly not welcome in that church.

At one point our church ran low on funds and a
group of local white business people got together and

formed a trust fund to help us out. It was considered
to be an act of charity and kindness, although many
of us recognized that these business people were more
interested in insuring that black people wouldn't try to
get into their own churches.

We all ran in our family. Howard and I ran for our school
track teams. All of us – Howard, Marjorie, Victor, and me
– ran in the races at the Labor Day picnic at Dundurn
Park, where the winners received baskets of groceries.
That picnic, one of many community events, was always
a highlight of the summer. Across the park there were
picnic tables laden with food. In the air was the smell of
good cooking. In the background, ships cut across the
blue water of Hamilton Harbour. And, of course, games
and races took place. Everybody knew our family and
they knew that when it came to athletics, we were tops.

"The Lewises are always sure to eat well because they
always go home with the groceries," people said. Those
groceries were a godsend to us, because my father, though
he worked hard all of his life, was just able to keep things
going on his annual income of about $1100.

CHAPTER 2

MY ROOTS

◆

My mother Emma was born in Collingwood, Ontario,
at the south end of Georgian Bay. My father Cornelius
was born in Simcoe, a southwestern Ontario farming
community. Both were descended from slaves who came
to Canada from the U.S. via the Underground
Railroad. Using the Underground Railroad and other
routes, thousands of blacks settled in southern Ontario
in the years leading up to the American Civil War.

Mary-Anne, my maternal grandmother, escaped with
her aunt from Charleston, South Carolina, in 1858.
Mary-Anne had a light complexion. Her aunt, also light
complexioned and passing as white, spirited Mary-Anne
across the border at Fort Erie, taking her first to Barrie
and then to Collingwood. Fort Erie was a popular
crossing place for blacks escaping slavery, as were
Windsor, Amherstburg, and Niagara Falls.

South Carolina was a horrible place for black people,
right up to the Civil War. It was a center of commerce
and the slave industry for close to 200 years. While I can't
be absolutely certain, my grandmother may have been the

property of the well-known Ball family. One of the Ball
family descendants, Edward Ball, wrote a book called
Slaves in the Family about their lives and experiences.

Slaves in those days were sometimes sent to the
Charleston Work House, a brick building that sat on the
outskirts of the town, where slaves were whipped, beaten,
and sometimes mutilated. Slaves were separated from
their families. They were worked hard in the fields from
dawn to sundown, and given little rest and the poorest of
food to eat. And yet they survived. Many of them, like my
grandmother, made the long trek northward to Canada.

Once across the border, they were free and instantly
became British citizens. Many famous African-Americans,
such as Reverend Josiah Henson, came to Canada and
settled in southwestern Ontario. In his autobiography,
Henson wrote of coming across the border and instantly
falling to the ground and kissing the earth of his new land
of freedom – that's how happy he was to be here.

My paternal great-grandfather, Isaac Gray, came to
Canada in 1855 and settled in Otterville, Ontario, a
village south of Woodstock. While I never found out
what part of the U.S. he came from, Isaac entered Canada
with his wife Elizabeth and several children. My paternal
grandmother, also named Elizabeth, was the oldest child.

Otterville was founded in 1807 and was the site of a
mill that sparked growth and moderate prosperity in the
community. The Otterville Mill, built ten years before
my great-grandfather arrived, still stands and is one of

the oldest continuously operating water-powered mills in
Canada. Otterville was a station on the Grand Trunk
Railway Line in the 1800s, and a prosperous place at the
time, with a bank, several churches, and a park that were
the focus of many community activities. Today, Otterville
is mainly a tourist destination.

Isaac soon put his skills to work in Otterville. At the
time, black men could usually find work only in barbering
or the building trades, such as carpentry and plastering.
Many former slaves were highly skilled builders, because
they had to construct and repair houses and farm buildings
on the plantations in the southern U.S. In 1855, Isaac
built the first African Methodist Episcopal church in
Otterville. With his family, he cleared land and built
homes and farm buildings for himself and his children.
Isaac also became a farmer.

The Civil War, though fought many miles to the
south, was well known in Otterville. And its outcome
forced some changes in Otterville's black community,
which by the mid-1860s had a school in addition to the
AME Church. Following the conclusion of the Civil War,
many in the Otterville Black Settlement decided to return
to the United States. But even after others in Otterville's
Black Settlement left for the U.S., Isaac and his family
stayed on.

Isaac Gray's daughter Elizabeth grew up and married
James Lewis, a barber who came from the U.S., though I
never found out the date. They had two boys and one girl.

My grandfather James, like other skilled tradespeople of his time, advertised in the local publication, the *Oxford and Norfolk Directory*. Underneath an advertisement for the "Simcoe And Paris Express and Daily Stage Line, Distance, 28 Miles," is an entry for "James Lewis, Barber & Hair Dresser." Below his address on Peel Street in Simcoe, C.W. (Canada West), it reads: "Also, Dealer in Hair Dye, &C., and Manufacturer of Lewis' Hair Lustre, which is the best article in use for removing Dandruff and beautifying the hair."

Discrimination against black people was very open in Canadian society when my father was growing up. But, he was a hard worker and wouldn't let it get him down. Everyone in my father's family had a knack for building things and my dad inherited that skill. But like many young black men, he was unable to find a job. From his birthplace in the farm country of southwestern Ontario, he traveled from town to town, looking for work and taking whatever job he could get. He eventually made his way to Hamilton where he met my mother, who worked as a maid for a family in the city of Guelph. My parents were married on July 4, 1900, at St. Paul's African Methodist Episcopal Church.

In those days, discrimination against black people was often worse if someone had very dark skin. My father had a very dark complexion and he found job-hunting tough. Many blacks could find jobs only as janitors, laborers, waiters, or maids. At one time my father found work in

Hamilton on a construction site as a hod carrier. A hod is
a tray used to carry mortar or bricks. My father was
strong, and worked diligently carrying the mortar and
bricks from the big tray where the mortar was mixed to
the bricklayers, who worked high up in the building.

Everything went well until he was told to leave the
job by the foreman, who discovered that the bricklayers
were dropping bricks from up above, trying to hit my
father on the head. The foreman figured it was only a
matter of time before my father was either knocked out
or killed by one of the bricks.

He later found work as a dining car waiter on the
Grand Trunk Railway, which ran from Chicago, Illinois,
across Ontario and into Quebec at Montreal, and then
into the United States to Portland, Maine.

After that he worked as a janitor for the Canadian
Westinghouse Corporation, part of the Westinghouse
Electric Company, which was started in 1886 by George
Westinghouse. Westinghouse was an American engineer
and inventor who designed and manufactured many
devices, including generators and electric motors. Today
the company is involved in many industries, including
nuclear power.

My father was one of only a handful of black people
working at Westinghouse, and there were no black
men working on the production side in the Westinghouse
plant until World War II. Every day, my father would
head into the plant, with his broom and mop ready, and

clean the floors, the washrooms, and the manufacturing
areas until they shone, all for no more than twenty-two
dollars a week. While that kind of money doesn't seem
like much, it allowed our family to buy a house. My
mother also brought money into the family from a job
scrubbing floors in restaurants.

Later on my father found work as a janitor with the
Canadian Porcelain Company, which manufactured
the porcelain insulating caps that sat on top of electrical
power lines. In addition to his janitor's job, he also developed blueprints for the company.

His ability to read and understand technical material,
in addition to his work skills, impressed the owners of the
company, who hired him as a handyman at their home. My
father was 84 when he died as a result of a heart attack.
My mother would live several years longer. She died at
age 88 in 1963, one week after the assassination of U.S.
president John F. Kennedy, someone who had done a great
deal to advance the rights of blacks in the United States.

I had learned much about my ancestors through my
parents. And I always enjoyed being able to pass on that
information to other family members. In 1982, shortly
after officiating at the unveiling of a cairn at the African
Methodist Episcopal Cemetery in Otterville during the
village's 175th anniversary, I found the gravesite of Isaac
Gray in a cemetery on Highway 59; he had died at age
75. Not long ago I took a young relative there and showed
her the gravestone.

"Who is that?" she asked.

"Your great-great-great-grandfather," I replied. She was impressed. I was pleased, too, that I was able to provide her with a link to our past.

CHAPTER 3

RACISM

❖

*Sometimes there's no nice way to approach a subject.
You just have to start talking about it and hope
that people will understand what you're talking
about and what the subject means to you. Racism is
just such a topic.*

The slavery that existed in Europe and North America
from the 1600s until the end of the Civil War began with
the English, who sought cheap labor for their plantations
in the West Indies. At the time, white people considered
non-white people to be inferior to them and they used
this justification as an excuse to keep them enslaved. In
fact, in the late 1700s, a German scientist named Johann
Blumenbach created a system that categorized people. He
placed white people, whom he called Caucasians (because
they came from the Caucasus Mountains in Russia), at the
top of his chart. At the bottom, he placed Africans. In
the middle he placed native North Americans, people
from Asia, and people from the islands in the South Pacific
Ocean. As a scientist, Blumenbach never considered that
he was doing anyone any harm, as he maintained that he

was simply putting people into categories based on how they looked. Yet, white Europeans and their descendants used this system as a means of justifying their poor treatment of non-white people for centuries. And they attached their own sets of negative attitudes, or stereotypes, to people based on skin color.

Slaves were brought by ship across the Atlantic Ocean, primarily from West Africa, and sold in North America in open marketplaces, the same way that someone might offer cattle for sale at a farmers market. Many native people in the U.S. were also captured and used as slave labor. With chains attached to their feet, slaves were sold to the highest bidder. Torn from their homeland, slaves were forced to work hard and were held against their will. Very often, they were sold away from their mothers, fathers, and siblings.

There were many white people who objected to slavery. The Quakers, for instance, were adamantly against slavery. The Quakers' religious beliefs stressed pacifism and they fought for the freedom of blacks in the U.S. for a century before the Civil War. They were also instrumental in helping many escaped slaves find freedom in Canada.

In Canada, Sir John Graves Simcoe, the first Governor of Upper Canada (which later became Ontario) attempted to outlaw Canadian slavery in 1793. While slave owners were against it, Governor Simcoe ensured that, over time, slavery would come to an end, by making any slave free upon reaching his or her twenty-fifth

birthday. Some Canadians used slave labor on their farms.
But slavery never became as big an industry in Canada
as it was in the U.S. In Canada, slavery was officially
outlawed in 1834, as it was outlawed in all British colonies
at the time.

In the mid-1800s, slaves who wanted to escape from
the southern United States faced a tough, long trek to
freedom in Canada. Many relied on the Underground
Railroad, which was not a railroad at all but a series of
safe places to hide: old houses, sheds, farm buildings,
and forests.

In 1850, the American government passed the Fugitive
Slave Law Act. That Act allowed bounty hunters to
capture escaped slaves in the northern "free states" of the
U.S. It also ensured that anyone hiding a slave would be
prosecuted under this law. Still, more than 3000 slaves
escaped to Canada within the first three months after the
law was passed. And, over the next ten years, more than
15,000 slaves would find freedom in Canada.

Harriet Tubman guided many slaves to freedom along
the Underground Railroad. Tubman was a famous former
slave who became very active in helping slaves escape.
She operated from the Ontario town of St. Catharines,
near the U.S. border. From 1851 to 1858, Tubman made
almost 20 trips to the U.S. and guided more than 200
slaves to freedom. At one time, she even had a $40,000
price placed on her head. She was renowned for being
very strong and tough, and she demanded that people
follow her orders from their starting point in the southern

states, through journeys of hundreds of kilometers north, often following the North Star as a guide, until they reached the Canadian border.

The slaves who escaped and came north to freedom created lives for themselves in hundreds of communities, not only in Ontario but in the Maritimes as well, especially Nova Scotia. They became farmers, bricklayers, teachers, lawyers, and politicians. They often established their own farming colonies where they would trade with other settlements.

The American Civil War was fought in the United States between 1861 and 1865. It was a conflict between the southern states that wanted to maintain slavery and the northern states that had already freed the slaves and were looking to ensure their freedom in every part of the country. Families were split apart because of their beliefs and many people died as they took up sides on either the southern Confederate Army or the northern Union Army. The war became famous for then-President Abraham Lincoln's Emancipation Proclamation, which officially freed the slaves on January 1, 1863.

It must be noted that, though they were free following the Civil War, blacks were rarely treated with respect. For instance, the year the Civil War ended, six Confederate soldiers created an organization called the Ku Klux Klan. These soldiers were angry over the new freedom enjoyed by former slaves. And they were afraid that black people would begin to compete with white people for jobs and education. As well, the Ku Klux Klan was against Roman Catholics and anyone who might oppose their views. Their goal was to strike terror into the hearts and minds of black people and anyone who supported the cause of equality. The Klan members wore long white robes and pointed hoods, and would ride their horses through the night, beating and sometimes hanging black men from trees, as well as burning crosses on the property of those who disagreed with them. In some places, lynchings were so popular that people would take photographs and make postcards of them to sell to others – even while the dead body was still swinging in the air. Blacks and many whites were terrified of the Klan.

Although it was created in the southern U.S. state of Tennessee, the Ku Klux Klan spread across the U.S. and into Canada. Many Klan members would parade openly in towns and cities, taking advantage of the fact that, even if some white people didn't agree with them openly, they often held similar attitudes towards non-white people.

By the 1920s, the Klan was a regular part of life in several Canadian communities. One day in 1929, my sister Marjorie came home from her job at an electrical firm with some unsettling news. A young white man who worked there as a janitor told her that on Friday night the Ku Klux Klan was going to burn a cross on Hamilton Mountain, the rising abutment of escarpment rock that marks the southern end of the City of Hamilton.

He warned her, whether out of genuine concern or
as a veiled threat, that "you and your family had better
be careful."

That Friday night about nine o'clock, a friend and
I were walking along Barton Street. As we crossed
Ferguson Avenue, we looked to the south, towards
Hamilton Mountain. There it was – a tall wooden cross
burning in the dusk.

"Look at that," my friend said to me, nudging my
arm. The cross was driven into the dirt and grass on a rise
of land, in a place where the local road curved around
Hamilton Mountain. The Klan members had driven
there, stopped their truck, wedged the kerosene-soaked
cross into the earth, set a torch to it, and driven off. The
arms of the cross glowed red in the twilight, against a sky
that was gradually lengthening into the purples and blues
of the night. Yellow flames leaped into the darkening
sky as we stood and stared at it. There were no arrests
that night for inciting hatred. There was no outcry from
the community. People went about their business as if
nothing significant had happened. From the balcony of
my home today, I can still see the spot where that cross
burned for hours on end. That cross burning was the first
I had seen of the Klan and its actions, though I would
often read accounts of their other campaigns of hatred
against black people.

In a way, the burning of the cross was anticlimactic
for me. Seeing it didn't create an overwhelming sense of
terror, because I already had an idea of what the Klan was

all about, and I already faced racism just about every day of my life. So it wasn't a surprise that some white people would take their cowardly hatred a further step, cover themselves with white sheets, and make a public display of their ignorance.

Months later, there was a Klan march through Hamilton. It was a big parade and the KKK rode through on horses. Even the horses wore white robes. The police did nothing to break up the event as the Klan members rode through a largely Italian neighborhood, trying to frighten the locals with their anti-Catholic views. Ironically, some of the horses, which were on loan to the Klan, were recognized as the property of a local bread company, even under their robes! As a result, many people boycotted the bread company and forced it out of business within a year.

While the Ku Klux Klan practiced extreme violence and advocated hatred against people, many white people practiced regular discrimination against black people every day, treating them like second-class citizens.

When I was a child, skin color was a major social issue. In many ways it still is; but back then you were reminded of your color – and the values people attached to it – regularly. How you were treated was as much based on how you looked as it was based on who you were inside. Getting a job, renting an apartment, shopping in certain stores, going to a restaurant – it all depended on your skin color.

The famous civil rights leader Dr. Martin Luther King Jr., in a speech delivered in 1963, said that he had a dream – "a dream that my four little children will one day live in a nation where they will not be judged by the color of their skin, but by the content of their character." The sadness of growing up in the early 20th century was that you were judged first, and sometimes only, on the color of your skin. The sadness, too, is that in many ways, this is still true.

I grew up being called a "colored boy." Today, we say someone is black – or African-Canadian, or "a person of color" – if his or her skin is not light.

As I grew up, "colored boy" would change to other terms; there was "Negro," which was a generally accepted term. There were also terrible names like "black bastard" and "nigger." That last one, what we often call "the N-word" today, is a painful, horrible word that carries within it a great deal of hate.

It hurts me today when I see rap or hop-hip artists and others using this word almost as a term of friendship or toughness. When I hear of young black men using it that way, I think they've lost sight of our history. For me, it never meant anything but hatred. When it was directed at my friends or me, I knew it was meant to hurt us and put us down. It dates back to the days when black people were slaves whose suffering and work were used to build great fortunes for slave owners.

The pain of being discriminated against was often, though not always, felt by the black community.

Sometimes comments, about me, members of my family, or friends, would come as casually as if a person were talking about the weather. But when the horrible words came, they rained down on me like hailstones. And like being caught in the hail, I often wanted to just run for cover.

"He's an uppity nigger," a white person might say about a black person, tossing off the remark as if they knew who we were inside, when they didn't really know at all. Other comments were filled with hatred and a desire to cause others pain.

When the racist comments came, we knew that the thoughts behind them were the same. We were stereotyped: white people had created their own ideas about blacks and then tried to make the reality fit their own ideas. They thought they knew what kinds of food we ate, without sitting down to eat with us; thought we were lazy, without seeing how hard we could work; thought we were stupid, without watching us work hard in school and study at home.

There was a lot of anger and hostility directed at black people, who lived and worked in a different class in society, though our society's laws and morals told us, over and over again, that we were equal.

When I was a child, I would get along with other kids on an equal basis. We might get into scraps or fights at school and not worry about being treated differently if we were punished. But something happens between childhood and adulthood. As they got older, black kids learned that there was less opportunity to fight back against the discrimination they felt every day.

If you were a young adult, fighting back could mean getting arrested. It could mean getting beaten up. It could mean a visit from the Ku Klux Klan. Almost an entire society was against us. And yet we had to learn to cope, live and raise families within that society.

It was that way not only for the black community in Hamilton but for others, too. In many housing sub-divisions in Hamilton, people would not sell to blacks, Jews, Italians, Russians, Turks, and others – in fact, it was often written into their sales agreements. In the work-place, blacks were prevented from working in factories or from joining unions.

When faced with daily discrimination, most black people took one of three approaches. We might become angry and hostile, and challenge white authority. We might learn to hide our feelings while in white society and become skilled at cloaking our emotions in the face of racism. Or, thirdly, we might learn to practice a forceful but diplomatic questioning of attitudes, based on the rights to equality that we had been promised. Sometimes, though rarely, one or more of us would cross the color barrier and marry a white person, defying society's anger.

When I was a child, I was regularly invited to birthday parties for my young white classmates and friends. The invitations lasted until I was about ten or eleven. After that, they dwindled until, by my teens, I was no longer invited to any functions with white people. It was when black children became teenagers that many white adults began to fear us. Their set of racist attitudes would kick in – and so they would prevent their own children from gaining the opportunity to recognize us not for how we looked but for who we were. They would pass their stereotypes on to their children, the way someone might hand down a family heirloom.

Beside my siblings, there was only one other black youngster that I recall during my elementary school years, a fellow named Ewan Bell. I never talked to Ewan about his experiences, but I think they were likely similar to mine.

Most of the time, other kids didn't bother me, but there was a kid named Reggie who would make racist comments to me occasionally, calling me a nigger. But, like most kids, Reggie and I would get into a scrap, pound on each other and then forget about it and become friends again . . . until the next time he made that mistake. Despite the occasional fisticuffs, we established a rough-and-ready friendship that can only come from the short and forgiving memories of children.

There was a time, however, when the impact of racism became deeply ingrained in me. One day I went by Reggie's home and called to him from the street. I was twelve years old.

"Reg! Reg!" I called. "Come on out and play!"

The front window of his house was open. I could hear his mother speaking to him in a voice tinged with hatred.

"I told you not to play with that nigger!" she said. "I don't want you playing with a colored boy."

Those words burned into me. The memory of them is as fresh, sore, and stinging as a skinned knee; it is as if it had happened yesterday.

It became clear to me that Reggie's racism had been learned. And it was even more painful because Reggie and his parents, being from southern Europe, were fairly dark-skinned too. There may have been places in Hamilton where they, because of their background, would not be allowed to purchase a house. And yet, because they were technically white, they fell into the pattern of racism that marked my city.

While playing with other kids, my race would come up in various ways, mostly subtle – other kids wanting to remind themselves that I was colored and they were white, seeking some consolation or affirmation that they were somehow superior to me.

I dealt with racism by standing up for myself. My parents, being very religious, would have told me to kneel down and pray. I would never say that their approach wasn't the right one. My parents dealt with the racism they encountered by finding inner strength in their religious beliefs. But, even as a youngster, I believed in being confrontational, mainly because I had nothing to lose by it. And if I were on the losing end of a battle, I was always certain to be able to outrun my opponent.

CHAPTER 4

RUNNING FAST

◆

*Running, and running fast – whether to make it
to school before the bell rang or to leave my classmates
in the dust in a race – came naturally for me.
At Wentworth Public School I began my track-
and-field career, guided by the very fine efforts of
our coach, Sergeant-Major McIntosh. A small,
squarely built man, he was a former soldier and
a fine coach who knew how to coax good performances
from young people.*

Sergeant-Major McIntosh lived in Bartonville, in the east
end of Hamilton, and came to our school once a week to
teach physical education. He was a wonderful man and he
inspired me as a sprinter.

"I've seen many a great sprinter in my time, and I've
coached a few too. And you've got the ability to be a fine
sprinter, Ray," he told me in his gentle Scottish brogue,
putting his hand on my shoulder.

It was a warm day in the spring. The sunshine poured
over the schoolyard and a cool, refreshing breeze blew
across the blades of grass, bending their tops down. In the

background was a rich wash of familiar sounds: the
rumble and *clickety-clack* of the streetcar and the *clop-clop*
of horses' hooves. The voices of people in the street
joined together in a jumbled chorus. Not far away, the
smokestacks of big companies like the Dominion Steel
Foundries billowed with smoke. Workers in coveralls,
their arms and faces marked by the grime and dirt of their
work, entered and exited the factories that huffed and
puffed like solid brick dragons, belching smoke and
spitting out iron.

Every day, I not only saw the way the white community had treated my family and others in the black
community, I had lived it. In a world where there was
very little in the way of inspiration coming from white
people, the words of this white man filled me with hope.
It was like a promise that a dream could come true, if I
had the strength to chase after and capture that dream.

"You have the discipline, the talent, and the heart to
do well for your community, and maybe our country
too," said the Sergeant-Major, and I knew when he said
"community," he meant the city of Hamilton, not just
Hamilton's black community. "Work hard and you'll be
able to do just about anything in track-and-field." Even at
age ten, I took the Sergeant-Major's words to heart. I was
determined to be the best runner possible.

There was no track at the school, so we ran in the
schoolyard. At that elementary level, we were strictly
sprinters. Up and down the schoolyard we would run in
short, fast sprints, the Sergeant-Major keeping track of

our times with his watch. Later on, we would train at
nearby Scott Park, a stadium that was fairly new at the
time. We also trained at the (91st Regiment) James
Street Armouries. In the mid-1920s, a wooden track was
installed at the Armouries, primarily to accommodate the
training of the great runner from Finland, Paavo Nurmi,
who was visiting our city.

The desire to run was like a fire inside of me. Just
about every day, I ran against my friends in an impromptu
race that would take us around the block in our neighborhood, a distance of about 600 yards. It was during those
races that I really developed my ability as a quarter-mile
runner. We would start at my house on Clyde Street, race
down to Wright Avenue, then to Leaming Street, on to
Cannon Street, and back to Clyde Street. I always gave
my pals a head start of two lampposts, or about 60 yards.
I would watch as my friends lit out down the street, then I
would take off. I could give them that much of a handicap,
10 percent of the distance, and still catch up to them and
pass them. Finally, I would come pounding around the
corner, my arms swinging slightly, head held high, to stop
in front of my house, victorious every time, my friends
trailing behind me.

"How did you do that, Ray?" they would ask. Catching
my breath, hands on hips, I would look up and reply, "I
don't know. I just like to run."

At Wentworth Public School I developed some
lasting friendships. At age ten, for instance, I ran against
Eddie Dore, who went on to become one of Hamilton's

leading dentists. We were friends for seventy years until his death from Lou Gehrig's Disease. In contrast to my relationship with some other white people, I'm happy to say that, throughout our long association, there was never an ill word between Eddie and me. And later on, I was glad to have a chance to speak to the last graduating class at Wentworth Public School the year it officially closed down in the 1970s.

Despite the fact that I was the only member of my family who would go on to win major track-and-field championships, my brother Howard was always our family's top runner. Along with Sergeant-Major McIntosh, Howard inspired me to run track-and-field.

I began running competitively when I was ten years old, and won my first award in 1920 for running at the Broadview YMCA Fall Fair in Toronto, competing in the 75-pound class.

In 1923, at age twelve, I traveled with Sergeant-Major McIntosh and the rest of our school's track team, to Montreal, where our team won a relay race at Molson Stadium.

Molson Stadium was the first place I ran in front of a large crowd. That excursion was also my first time traveling on a train. All of the team members, including my buddies on my relay team – Ken Hales, Jack Gorman, and Tom Harkness – were excited about going to Montreal. We traveled in a sleeper car, a special train car equipped to allow passengers to enjoy the passing scenery during the day before being converted to sleeping compartments at night.

There was one stickler to me competing in Montreal, however. You had to be thirteen years old, and I was still twelve, my birthday being a few months away. That was less of a problem for Sergeant-Major McIntosh than it was for me; the Sergeant-Major told the organizers that I was already thirteen, allowing me to compete.

At Molson Stadium, the race itself was fast and furious. I remember the heat of the day beating down on me. The crowds in the stands and on the sidelines cheered us on. I recall waiting at my mark on the track, watching my teammates race around the track – their legs pumping, arms swinging – looking at the baton bobbing up and down, getting closer and closer until the hand-off was made to me and I took off down the track. The lessons from my neighborhood training were deep inside of me. Even though a couple of runners were ahead, I soon passed them, my heart thumping, until I crossed the finish line, bringing my team the first-place finish.

The victory photograph of me, along with Ken, Jack, and Tom, winners of the relay race, hung for many years in the halls of Wentworth Public School. My brother Howard, sixteen years old at the time, also competed at the same meet and won the Ontario Schoolboy Championship for the 100-yard dash.

My father never saw me run; he wasn't a very sports-minded person, although earlier in my life he sometimes watched Howard run. My mother also went to see

Howard run, but when the gun went off she would close
her eyes. She wouldn't open them again until she heard
his voice announced as a winner, which was almost a
certainty. I guess she was watching him race around the
track in her mind.

There was an excitement in running those races.
You wanted to win just because winning was the goal,
pure and simple. It was part of being a kid. And before
I became too aware of racism and the effect it had on
people, I was thrilled to be lining up against other boys
my age, watching them as they tried to psyche themselves
up for the competition. The feeling of surging forward
as the gun went off, head to head against the others, and
then pulling ahead of them as we raced down the track,
listening to their steady breathing and feeling my heart
leaping in my chest, gave me a shot of pure adrenaline
that would carry me all the way to the Olympics nine
years later.

CHAPTER 5

HIGH SCHOOL

◆

*By the time I entered Hamilton Central Collegiate
Institute, I could outrun just about anyone. And I was
certainly in the right place for competition, for the
school was famous for sending winning teams to track-
and-field events all over Canada and the United
States. I was determined to work hard and become a
member of our school's winning track team.*

One of the most popular events at the time was the
Penn Relays, held at the University of Pennsylvania in
Philadelphia. I had always wanted to go to this event and
knew I could do a good job if I could earn a place for
myself on the team.

My running abilities were well known to the coaching
staff at Central Collegiate. But I ran into problems with
the head of the physical education department, Captain
John Richard Cornelius, whom everyone called Cap. Like
my elementary school coach, Sergeant-Major McIntosh,
Cornelius was originally from Scotland, and had served in
the military. But that was where the similarity ended.
McIntosh was a gentle and kind man, whereas Cornelius

ruled the track with an iron hand. Nobody questioned his authority.

By the time I got to high school, Cap had already served a distinguished career in the military during World War I and was a professor of military science at Princeton University. He was considered to be one of the best track-and-field coaches anywhere in the world, and he would take Hamilton's top runners to the 1924, 1928, and 1932 Olympics. I would be among those runners at the 1932 Olympics.

Cap was very good at motivating students to run well – sometimes through fear, sometimes through positive motivation – and he always pushed them to their limits. He was a tall, lean man with a neatly trimmed moustache, his hair slicked back. Carrying himself with military precision, he would call out to the boys on the team: "You can do better than that!" And almost every time, they did. The runners would continually improve on their previous times. Most of Cap's techniques worked well, for he would guide Hamilton's top athletes for more than forty years.

But there was a dark cloud hovering over Cap, and by association over me. For he was a terrible racist and I felt his hatred towards black people every time I was in his presence.

Yet, those Penn Relays were like a magnet for me. I was anxious to find a place on the team. At the first team meeting to prepare for the Penn Relays, Cap had one of my fellow students read out a list of names of those who

would go to Philadelphia. We gathered around to listen
for our names.

"Only those named on the list should come out
for practice, because Captain Cornelius is going to be
very busy getting the boys ready for the team," the
student said.

My name was never mentioned. I knew Cap didn't
want me on the team, because several times he had made
the remark that he "couldn't take the team to Philadelphia
with a colored boy on it." For Cap, that was the end of the
matter. I wasn't named for the team. So I wouldn't run.

It was 1927. I would be turning seventeen in a few
months, and blacks were only just beginning to earn
respect for their athletic abilities on mostly white
sports teams. African-Americans were creating black
baseball teams in the Negro Leagues in the U.S., and
many African-Canadians would play in those leagues.
Groups like the Colored Intercollegiate Athletic
Association were beginning to make track-and-field
popular among African-American athletes, and there
were great African-American sprinters like Eddie Tolan
and Ralph Metcalfe. As individuals, blacks were becoming
established as boxers and football players. The great
African-American actor, Paul Robeson, made a name for
himself as a football player in college. The first African-
American basketball team, the Renaissance Big Five, was
beating all-white teams.

But it wasn't until after World War II that efforts were
made to integrate blacks into white-dominated sports

teams, and in many parts of the U.S. integrated
sports teams would be illegal until the 1950s. In 1947,
Jackie Robinson broke major league baseball's color
barrier. In the National Basketball Association in 1950,
Chuck Cooper and Sweetwater Clifton quietly erased
that invisible line.

But back in the 1920s it was a different story. Cap's
all-white world was very normal for society. For a young
black man, being part of a team, any team, was an uphill
battle. And it was a battle that I was determined to win.

When I was barred from the team, my friends wanted
to take the matter to the principal and argue on my behalf.
But I was determined to prove Cap wrong to leave me
out – and I wanted to do it in my own way. World-famous
coach or not, Cap's racist attitude lit a fire inside me.

On my own, I trained to get ready for an upcoming
event, the 91st Regiment Indoor Meet at the James Street
Armouries. I prepared to run in the 60-yard dash and the
300-yard run for boys eighteen and under. I easily won
both events. I knew that, in the minds of track-and-field
coaches across the city, the decision by Cap to keep me
off the team because of my color would be seen as a bad
one to make.

The coach wasn't the only person who proved a challenge
in school. A teacher, Robert Hunter, was also a racist.
Mr. Hunter was an Olympian himself, having won a silver
medal at the 1924 Paris Olympics as part of the rowing
team. He was big man – about six feet, four inches tall –

and still carried himself like a standout athlete. As a
teacher, he, like Cap, commanded absolute authority.

One occasion I remember well was in study hall,
where several students and I were working on homework.
The supervising teacher was Mr. Hunter. Occasionally,
there were undoubtedly whispered conversations back
and forth, as students have always had. When this happened, Mr. Hunter told us to be quiet. Then he pointed
at me, though I was not the guilty student and had been
quiet the whole time.

Ordering me out of the room, he slapped me hard
on the back of my head as I passed by. Angry, I turned to
him. I put my index finger up to him and said, "Don't you
ever do that to me again!" Later that day my friends told
me that, after I had left the classroom, Hunter was
incensed and had called me a "low-down dirty nigger . . .
the scum of the earth."

I took my complaint to the principal, Mr. Morris.
Morris called Hunter into his office. We sat for a few
minutes, me angry and looking down at the floor.

"Did you send this student out of your class, then hit
him as he left?" the principal asked. Hunter came out
strongly against me.

"Lewis was talking and disrupted my class," he said,
his eyes angry. He stabbed a finger in the air. "I have
a right to throw out a student who disrupts my class,
don't I?"

It wasn't really a surprise to me that Mr. Morris
accepted Hunter's explanation. But before I left the room,

I regained my composure and looked Hunter in the eyes.

"You have just lost your manhood today," I said to him. "You're no longer a man in my eyes." Hunter, a great Olympian and representative of Canada only a few years earlier, was downcast. He shifted uncomfortably but, with the principal present, wasn't about to physically retaliate. Of course, I was also disappointed in Mr. Morris, who was normally a decent person. By not supporting me or even considering my side of the story, he simply toed the line on white attitudes towards black people. Too often, white people would turn a blind eye to unfairness and injustice.

CHAPTER 6

THE PENN RELAYS

◆

*Back in the area of track-and-field, I was one of
many young black men who were finding ways to
express themselves as athletes. In addition to achieving
our goals of athletic excellence, young black men
found that, in a society that was too often against us,
track-and-field was a place where we could compete
equally with white people. Nobody could argue with
a stopwatch or make excuses or accusations – if you
were the better runner, that was that, and there
were no questions asked.*

As the Penn Relays approached, I kept myself focused on
my goal of eventually, somehow, making the team. At the
time my brother Howard, who was always the best runner
I ever saw, was also very well-known in the Hamilton athletic community. He was on track to make the Canadian
team for the 1928 Olympics but, with economic times
difficult and the Great Depression approaching, he was
more focused on finding a job than on running track.
Eventually he would become disillusioned with society
and hang up his track shoes forever.

But before he quit, Howard had his local fans. They included M.M. "Bobby" Robinson. Robinson was a popular sports reporter and editor with the *Hamilton Spectator* newspaper, who helped to raise money for our school through the On to Philly Fund. Always a great organizer of sports in Hamilton, Robinson was the creator of the modern British Empire Games, which became the Commonwealth Games. Today, there is a high school in Burlington named after him and he's also a member of Canada's Sports Hall of Fame.

The idea for the British Empire Games began with the Reverend J. Astley Cooper, who promoted his idea in a British magazine in 1891. Cooper's proposal was to hold a festival that would bring British subjects, many of them spread out across the world, closer together. In 1911 a Festival of the Empire was held at the Crystal Palace in London, England, as part of the coronation of King George V. Canada won a silver cup competing in track-and-field, boxing, wrestling, and swimming against competitors from South Africa and Australia. But World War I would soon intervene.

In the 1920s, under the persistence of Robinson, the idea was revived. Robinson was smart and ambitious, and really wanted Canada, and in particular Hamilton, to have the spotlight of international competition shine on it.

Robinson's ideas came at the right time, too, for Hamilton was likely *the* home of track-and-field in Canada during the 1920s. The Hamilton Olympic Club, for instance, would organize Twilight Meets on Wednesday

nights. For 25 cents, fans could come out and see the
best runners from clubs in Hamilton, Toronto, and
elsewhere. More than 2000 fans would fill the stands
for those meets.

In 1928, Robinson was manager of Canada's track-
and-field team at the Amsterdam Olympics, and began
talking with officials about holding a sports event in
Hamilton in 1930. The event became a reality, and competitors came from Australia, Bermuda, British Guiana,
England, Ireland, New Zealand, Newfoundland (at that
time independent of Canada), Scotland, South Africa, and
Wales. Ever since, the games have been held every four
years at the midway point between Olympic Games.

Robinson was very influential in Hamilton's sporting
community and had watched me run several times. The
Hamilton Spectator sponsored our team for the Penn
Relays. After a local meet, he approached me and asked
why I wasn't on the team that was going to Philadelphia.

"Cap left me off the team," I told him. That was
enough information for Robinson. Robinson was a tough
man, with a bit of a temper. After our talk, he called the
school and spoke with Cap personally.

"If Ray doesn't go, the team doesn't go," he said to
Cap. "Ray is one of the anchors that makes this a competitive team. He's *got to be a part of it.*"

Cap was also tough. He was adamant about keeping
me off the team. And I stayed off the team. But true to his
word, Robinson managed to cancel the team's trip to the
Penn Relays.

Society was difficult for blacks. But it was also tough for others, including Italians and Jews. Italians, many of them immigrants, were often given the hardest jobs at the lowest wages. People would spit on them in the street and call them names. A fellow student named Morris Levine, a Jew, who ran the mile relay and would later become a doctor, was one of the school's top runners and was better than some of the other boys who made Cap's team. Like me, Morris was left off the team by Cap. Cap's explanation was that, because the meet was being held on a weekend, "with their religious beliefs, [Jewish people] can't eat the same things that we eat on a Saturday, so he wouldn't run as well."

It was common for black and Jewish athletes to be denied opportunities to compete. And it makes me wonder how many good athletes were passed over because of ignorance – and how many schools passed up a chance to add trophies and medals to their collections because of prejudice.

So, while we didn't run in Pennsylvania, our team went instead to the Marquette University Relays in Milwaukee, Wisconsin. We won most of the races there. We went in 1927, 1928, and 1929.

In 1927, John Fitzpatrick, Hamilton Central Collegiate's top runner, graduated and I took his place as the school's top track-and-field athlete. In addition to competing at Marquette, I finally did win out against Cornelius and went to the Penn Relay competitions in 1928 and 1929 – and I still have the two gold watches I

won at those meets. I met the great sprinter Ralph
Metcalfe in Milwaukee, and we remained good friends for
many years. An African-American, Ralph was one of the
greatest American sprinters ever. He would go on to win
a gold medal at the 1936 Olympics in Berlin, Germany,
as a member of the U.S. 4x100-meter relay team, and he
won silver medals at the 1932 and 1936 Olympics in the
100-meter dash.

In 1928, before I had even turned eighteen, I tried to
qualify for the Canadian track-and-field team that would
go to the Olympics in Amsterdam. In the 400 meters, I
ran three qualifying races in a four-hour period. I finished
fourth and expected to get on the team, as the top four
runners were chosen to go.

Instead, they took a runner named Stan Glover. The
officials said they believed Stan could run a stronger race,
but I knew there was more to it than that – I was left off
Canada's 1928 Olympic team because of my color.

But my running continued to improve. In 1929, I
went to Philadelphia for a U.S. National Interscholastics
medley relay, where I came fifth in the 100-yard race and
second in the 220 yards. And what an atmosphere to run
in! The heat was so intense that it was 37° Celsius in the
shade, but I still managed to run six races in the space of
less than three hours.

Philadelphia was definitely *the* place to be as a runner.
In the Xmas 1929 edition of our school's yearbook, in the
Athletics section, writer Albert M. Pain wrote:

the goal of every boy who goes in for track
work at Central is to make the Philadelphia
team. The Philadelphia Relay meet is the
greatest meet of its kind in the world. Over 400
high schools and colleges are represented at
these races. A victory for any school in a relay
race there means that they are champions of
North America at that distance.

He later described my work in the mile relay at Philly:

Lewis, the lead-off man, was among the 17
who started for the various teams, each fighting
to be away first. Lewis, in his anxiety, broke
twice and was set back a yard. Even with this
handicap, he was off like a shot and was five
yards ahead at the 50-yard mark.

Our team ended up winning the race by 15 yards!
   The year 1929 was a monumental one for our track
team. We were winners at the Toronto Indoor Meet,
we did well at the Hamilton Indoor Meet, we won in
Philadelphia, and in Milwaukee that April I took two-
fifths of a second off the old record in the 100-yard dash.

It certainly was a different time. Track-and-field today is
much different. Today, you might run one or two races a
day. In the 1920s, it could easily be five or six races, with
very little time to rest or take on fluids.

In those days, we ran on cinder tracks outdoors. These tracks were often gouged out in places where athletes had dug in their toes for traction – sometimes they looked like horses had gone back and forth over them. The first rubber-based track would not be installed until 1950, and today there are a number of surfaces that athletes can run on, all of them weatherproof and more cushiony than the tracks of yesteryear. Indoors, we ran on hard wooden tracks. Today, the indoor tracks are spongy and easy on the feet.

In terms of money, today we have trust funds for amateur athletes that allow them to pursue their athletic goals. In my day, you made what money you could; you trained whenever you found time, and many athletes had part-time or full-time jobs to make ends meet.

Today, there is clothing that is lightweight and made of breathable materials. Years ago, we had cotton shorts and would run in sleeveless tank tops, what we referred to as "underwear" tops. And shoes? They're as different today as you can imagine – just walk into any athletic shoe store and look at the selection. Back then, we got by with two pairs of track shoes: one with longer spikes for outdoor running, the second with pin-size spikes for running on the wooden tracks indoors.

Today, runners have starting blocks that allow them to push off at the beginning of a race. When I ran – and right up to the 1960s – athletes dug out their own "starting blocks" in the cinder track.

Today, runners have masseurs, managers, coaches, and equipment specialists. In my day, you were lucky to have a coach that would spend time with you, telling you what you needed to change in order to run an effective race. When we ran, we watched our shadows in the sunlight, correcting our posture and the swing of our arms. Today, athletes are analyzed from a dozen different perspectives.

Nowadays, athletes warm up with loose jogging around the track, neck rolls, arm swinging and hip rolling to loosen up the joints, back and leg stretches, calf stretches, and bounding or leaping into the air while alternately thrusting the knees as high as possible. Today many athletes, especially sprinters, are heavily muscled in the chest and arms. They almost always have weight-lifting programs, whereas in my day, runners stayed away from weights. In my day, we started a workout with a few laps at a jogging pace around the track. We then worked into more intense, three-quarter speed runs before finishing with full-speed sprints. A practice might last two hours, and it was always focused on running, pure and simple. Rain or shine, cinder track or street, running was everything.

My last big hurrah in high-school track-and-field was at the Canadian High School Championships in Hamilton in 1929. It was held at the Hamilton Civic Stadium. I won four championships in one afternoon – I won the 100 yards, the 220 yards, and the 440 yards, and I anchored the mile relay. I ran a total of six races in one day.

Later that year, I was in Banff, Alberta, for the Canadian Nationals on Labor Day, where I would win the 440-yard race, also known as the quarter-mile. We arrived in Banff before the national championships began. On the Saturday, two days before Labor Day, another event, the Highland Games, was being held. We were invited to take part in the Highland Games as a tune-up for the Nationals, and our coaches advised us to pick the races in which we thought we could do well.

One of my teammates, Bernard Irwin, said he'd like to run the quarter-mile for the grand prize, which was a silver dinner service for six. Everyone on the team wanted that prize. We all figured we could win it. But we knew, too, that we were all pretty equally matched as runners. So we figured out an innovative way to determine which runner from our team might be given an opening to win the race. We tossed coins against the wall, and agreed that the one whose coin landed closest to the wall would be given room by his teammates to ease into first place and gain the prize. My coin came up closest to the wall. Bernard said, "Let's have one more toss, Ray." Again, we tossed our coins and I won.

That afternoon in the race, we rounded into the final turn and Bernard was ahead of me by about three yards. "Hey, Bern," I called out to him. He eased up to let me pass and win.

Two days later, at the National Championships on
Labor Day, I ran against Bernard in the quarter-mile and
won – earning the National High School title.

Those were exciting times. But track-and-field, whether
at a high-school stadium, at a university track center or,
later on, at the Olympics and British Empire Games, was
not my only forte.

I also played a season of football in high school. I
played the "end" position, a position that would eventually evolve into the wide receiver spot, but it was at a time
before the forward pass was added to the game. A team-
mate of mine, Vince Bryant, who was also black, would
line up next to me to receive the opposing team's kick-off,
and seven out of ten times we scored – we were that fast!

My most vivid, though not my most pleasant, memories of high-school football are from a championship
game played against Toronto's Bloor Collegiate. The star
of that team was a big, strong black player named Skanks.

Our football coach was a colorful local character
named Sam Manson. Manson ran a sporting goods store
and was a leading sports figure in Hamilton. Later on,
he became a city controller and an important figure in
local government, and served on the Hamilton Board of
Control. He was the manager of Canada's track-and-field
team that went to England for the British Empire Games
in 1934, and also managed the 1936 Canadian Olympic
team in Berlin. In football, he was captain of the Hamilton
Tigers when the team won its first Grey Cup. So you

might say Sam Manson was an extraordinary man –
yet, when he coached football, his attitude was typical
for the times.

Manson was incensed that Skanks was doing so well
against our team. Manson jumped up and down, screaming
at the top of his lungs, "Stop the nigger! Stop the nigger!"
Then he turned to me and, by way of apology, said "Sorry,
Ray, I just can't help it!" To my mind, he could have done a
lot better, if only to keep his true racist feelings to himself.

I felt anger and disappointment in Manson's attitude –
and I buried my feelings deep. But I couldn't play another
season of football under Coach Manson. Many years later
I ran into Manson when he was a politician. He asked
me what happened to the great American sprinter Ralph
Metcalfe. I told him Ralph was coaching at a black
Catholic university in New Orleans. Manson couldn't
believe that. "I didn't know there were any colored
Catholics," he exclaimed.

"You never know who you might meet," I replied.
"For instance, I would be glad to take you to New York
City where you can meet many black Jews."

Angry at my insolence, Manson replied, "We help your
church a lot!" He was referring to white business people
providing financial help to black churches in Hamilton.

"And so you should help us," I said, "Because you sure
don't give us any work."

And that was true – it was just as tough in the late
1920s for a black man to find work as it was back when
my father was looking for work in the late 1890s.

CHAPTER 7

BLACK LIFE IN HAMILTON IN THE 1920S

Life was always a struggle for my parents. Still, they scraped together what money they could to make improvements to our house. First, they raised the house on a brick foundation. They later added a dormer over the front door, and then created a screened-in porch. Later on, they added a bathroom inside the house. We were happy with that – no more using an outhouse! And finally, we covered the house with a weatherproof covering.

The folks next door were white and, while they were not overly friendly, we got along okay with them. But when my father built the screened-in, mosquito-free porch, while the man next door had to suffer with the mosquitoes in the summer, it was too much for him. He'd been raised to believe that white people were superior to blacks and he couldn't stand the idea that we had something better than he did.

This man was a custodian in a post office. He was also a Sunday school teacher. But he could not stand to see black people raise their standard of living, especially higher than his own. He would be out digging in his garden and cursing us. "Those black bastards, damn niggers," he would say, not too loud, but loud enough that we could hear him.

Another neighborhood incident involved the 25th wedding anniversary of the neighbors who lived behind us on the next street. Everybody in the neighborhood, except us – the black family – was invited to the party. When the anniversary celebrants offered a slab of cake to my mother over the back fence, my mother smiled right back at her. "Why don't you take it back and give it to one of the nice people who came to celebrate your big day?" she said, and walked away.

On another occasion, a white neighbor, Mrs. Jennings, knocked on our door with a petition to sign. "Hello, Mrs. Lewis. How are you today?" she said with a smile. "You know, Mrs. Lewis, the people across the street are selling their house, and they're selling it to foreigners. Now as you know, most of us don't want foreigners on Clyde Street."

My mother was never a liar. She attended church every week and always demanded that we be honest and truthful. But she sure served up a nice little fib that day – just to get back at Mrs. Jennings, whose bigotry demanded a lesson.

"You know, Mrs. Jennings," she said. "My sisters are considering moving to Hamilton and I was trying to find some property for them on Clyde Street. That house would be perfect. Absolutely perfect."

Mrs. Jennings was upset. She didn't want foreigners on Clyde Street, but she didn't want more black people either. "Well, Mrs. Lewis," she said quickly. "I really must go now." She took her petition and left.

There were few blacks in our neighborhood, but those of us there had pride in our roots. We stood up for ourselves. One neighbor I always remember was Mrs. Hughes. She was a former slave and, when I was a child, she was already seventy-five years old. She was bent slightly with age, but she had bright eyes, a keen wit, and a great memory of the past. Mrs. Hughes was very close to my mother and gave her an earthenware pot that she had brought with her from the U.S. when she escaped slavery.

You can imagine what it must be like to live your whole life in a country and yet be made to feel that you're not a part of it. That happened to me in Guelph in 1929. My friend Lloyd Johnson, also black, and I were there during a centennial celebration. A white man shoved us both off the sidewalk. We tumbled into the street. "Go back to where you came from, niggers!" he yelled at us. No one in the crowd came to our side.

I was angry. *Where would we go?* I thought to myself. *We're from here. We're Canadians! This is our country.*

Lloyd was mad, too, so mad that he wanted to get into a physical fight with the man. But I pulled Lloyd away, telling him that the next stop for us would be a jail cell – white people just didn't care about any injustice done to a black man.

The rules of social life in the 1920s and 1930s were strictly enforced – whites and blacks could play together on the same team, they could go to the same school, but they would rarely, if ever, socialize. I could not allow myself to be seen with a white girl, or else I would run the risk of being beaten up by an angry mob. The same would go for white people who tried to socialize with blacks. Society would not allow it.

In places like restaurants, or even social events like picnics, there were rules that kept the races separate. Blacks could eat in some restaurants, but not all. We could dance in some clubs, but not all. I found that out myself at La Salle Park in Burlington, when I attended a church picnic as a teenager.

The picnic had good food, lots of games and competitions, and plenty of socializing. *So far, so good*, I thought, until, later in the evening, I headed to the dance floor when the band started playing. I asked a pretty black girl to dance. Once on the floor, I felt a hard rap on my shoulder. I turned to see a commissionaire, a former military veteran who was hired to maintain security, staring at me. His face was red, his hair damp. It felt like his intense eyes were drilling a hole in me. "You can't dance here," he said.

"Why not?" I asked, though, looking around at the ocean of white faces around me, moving to the music, I already knew the answer.

"Because you just can't," he said. He took a half step towards me. "If you don't like it, you can leave. In fact, why don't you just leave?"

I left, my pride intact, but my anger – the same anger first lit by Captain Cornelius – burning inside me.

Things were indeed difficult, in social and economic circles. Still, while I was in high school I enjoyed my own little share of fame and celebrity. I had always received a good share of media coverage for my endeavors, though I was occasionally the victim of stereotyping by eager writers always ready to add more "color" to a story.

A *Hamilton Spectator* sportswriter, Ivan Miller, once approached me about a story in late 1929. I refused to talk to him, because of an earlier story he wrote about my performance at the U.S. high-school championships in Philadelphia. We had run in mud in Philadelphia; the steady downpour had made the track a path of filthy, soupy muck for three days. Nonetheless, the competitions went on, rain or shine. I had remarked to Ivan Miller that I was getting used to running in the mud.

When the story came out, Miller quoted me in the paper as saying that, when I ran, there wouldn't be a drop of mud showing on my shirt. But he also wrote it in a southern U.S. dialect, something that I knew nothing about, having been born and raised in Canada and grown up with a decidedly Canadian accent. Miller phrased my quote as, "No suh, they ain't goin' be no mud showin' on ma shirt, no suh, nun' t'all," or words to that effect. Like a lot of whites, Miller thought it a great joke to poke fun at my presumed background, as if I, along with every other black person, spoke in a lazy southern drawl. I made a point of never speaking to Miller again.

CHAPTER 8

AFTER HIGH SCHOOL

*I graduated on a hot and muggy day in June 1929.
I was pleased to have had such a great career in high
school. I was especially happy when I was informed
that I had won a scholarship to Marquette University.
It was well known as a top track-and-field school
and was run by Jesuit priests, who were known
for their strict discipline.*

I enrolled at Marquette in September 1929. My plans
were to continue to be a top competitor in Marquette's
track-and-field program. I had won the Nationals earlier
at Banff, Alberta, and had beaten Marquette's top quarter-
miler there. My track record was strong and proven, and
it drew the school to me.

I planned to study dentistry. Shortly after I arrived at
Marquette, I was called to the office of Father Grace, the
Dean of the College of Liberal Arts and Sciences. While
I sat in his office, Father Grace telephoned the Dean of
Marquette's Dental School. "I have a colored boy sitting
here with me, named Ray Lewis. Ray has been brought
in from Canada to run for the school," Father Grace

said. He chatted for a few minutes with the other Dean. Hanging up the phone, Father Grace turned to me with a smile. "If you're successful with your studies, Ray, you will be permitted to enter dental school."

I was ecstatic and set down to work hard in university. But it turned out to be a difficult time for me. I didn't have a lot of money and had to miss some meals. I couldn't run because regulations prevented freshmen from competing in the fall for the school. And I was months away from the beginning of the indoor season. I was anxious to get on with running and I missed my family. If I couldn't run for Marquette, I wanted to get back home to Canada and hopefully earn a place on the national team. By the end of the year, I had packed my bags and taken the train home to Hamilton.

I arrived home on Clyde Street during the Christmas season. Christmas lights were being hung. With the Great Depression coming, people were not too optimistic about the economy, and jobs were becoming scarce. Despite this, people were happy. Our street was a white sea of snow and ice; kids would lace up their skates and glide right down the street itself to the local parks to play hockey.

I was also optimistic. I had a high profile in track-and-field, and my name had been mentioned regularly in the sports section of the *Hamilton Spectator*. I was young and strong, and felt that my prospects of finding a job were good. For two years, the Otis Elevator Company had sponsored my running, and I had worked for that company for two summers. But a job I received with the

company on my return from Marquette lasted only a
month before I was laid off.

In high school, I had been a guest at many luncheons,
where white businessmen would slap me on the back,
smiling and laughing and trying to make me feel special.
They were the people who put money into Hamilton's
track-and-field programs. They wanted to be seen being
friendly to its top athletes, and they knew that runners
like me helped to promote their business.

"Ray, you are of a higher class than the American
Negroes we see," they would say to me. "We think you're
among the best at running, anywhere." Being young, I
almost believed it.

But now, out of school, out of work, and not running
in competition, I was ignored. I was just another black
person who was out of a job. When I ran in high school,
I had a profile. But now, white society tossed me into
the dustbin.

I looked around me. Other athletes, all of them white,
many of them not possessing a track record as good as
mine, were getting jobs. They became police officers,
firefighters, and recreational supervisors. I had to lace up
a new pair of shoes – work shoes – and begin pounding
the pavement as I knocked on doors for work.

I paid a visit to M.M. Robinson, the great sports
reporter at the *Hamilton Spectator*. Hadn't he supported
me only a few years ago, as I tried to get on the
high-school track-and-field team? I was certain he
might help.

Robinson's response was "Sorry, Ray. There's nothing for you here at the *Spectator*." But he was always a sportsman, and so it wasn't a surprise when he asked me when I would start training for the British Empire Games that he had created. He didn't seem to realize that I needed money, to buy food to eat, before I could think about running again. Robinson, like most whites back then, thought I was good for athletics only, and he certainly wanted me to help maintain Hamilton's shining image as the home of excellence in track-and-field.

I was angry at that attitude – for while I was recognized for my athletic abilities, no one would help me get a job. I did not try out for the Canadian team for the 1930 British Empire Games; instead, I began training on my own again. And looking for a job.

The few months after I arrived back in Hamilton were difficult. I expanded my job search and found my way to Toronto, where I got a job as a railway porter on the Canadian Pacific Railway in May 1930. The CPR had been in business, running trains across the country's transcontinental railway, since 1885. It was very successful at moving both products and people to destinations across Canada and into the U.S., and would go on to become a large and diversified company. When I joined, the company was in serious competition with Canada's other big railway company, the Canadian National Railway, or CNR.

It was the time of the Great Depression. Companies went bankrupt. People lost their jobs. So, in a way, those of us who could find jobs were lucky. A month after I got my job on the railway a new prime minister, Richard Bedford Bennett, took office, promising to do everything he could to end unemployment. While he was a generous man and would often give people money out of his own pocket, he was never successful at ending unemployment during his five-year term. Though eventually the economy improved, the Great Depression wouldn't officially end until World War II began in 1939.

Working as a porter was not a fun job. It was a job where you worked and worked hard. And it was a job that white people preferred to give to black men, for it cast us in the role of servant. So while we had jobs, we had to pay a price for it.

You can't imagine how many times, in movies and in plays, black actors were put in the position of playing servants. Blacks were prominent in advertising as janitors, maids, butlers, and waiters. Indeed, it was a fairly accurate reflection of how we were treated in the workplace. At the same time it should be understood that even though most of us had a hard time getting jobs, there were black professionals – teachers, doctors, accountants, lawyers, and dentists – who were very successful. But they were only a small minority in the overall population.

When I joined the CPR, I became part of a long and continuing tradition of black men serving white people on the trains that began after the invention of the sleeping car in the late 1850s by the American inventor George

Pullman. George Pullman went on to make a lot of
money with his invention. He has been seen in different
ways over the years, either as a criminal who abused his
black workers, paying them only half the money
white workers wanted, or as a hero who gave African-
Americans jobs that they desperately needed. Either
way, Pullman made the stereotype of the black man
as a servant stronger than ever in the minds of white
Americans and Canadians.

One of the things I had to buy before getting the job
was a shoeshine kit. I paid six dollars for it, and it contained two soft brushes and a dauber for applying the
shoe polish. They were good quality and I still have them
today, many years later. The company supplied the uniforms and we got our meals for half price.

As a porter, I made beds and shined shoes, provided
snacks and other light food to passengers, and mopped
the floors. Porters maintained the passenger cars in
spotless condition, as these cars were the pride of the
Canadian Pacific Railway. Each sleeping car contained ten
separate compartments, with upper and lower sections, or
berths, where people slept. Each compartment had its
own sink and a toilet, and was finely decorated. These
rooms could be opened up to other rooms if you had a
large group of people traveling together. There was also
a drawing room – kind of like a living room – at the end
of the car. It was bigger and could sleep three, had a sofa,
and was usually occupied by wealthy people or politicians.

The compartments had rich-looking wood paneling, often of mahogany. At one end of the hallway there was an additional washroom.

We porters had a small room at the end of the row. It contained a washbasin and a single bed. But privacy? Forget it! There was often just a thin curtain separating us from the hallway. People could holler out to us or even pull back the curtain to see if we were there.

I came into the porter's job as an outstanding high-school athlete with several national titles to my name. I had my name in the newspaper many more times than many of the people I would serve on the train. And yet, when I put on my uniform, I became just another black man serving the white traveler. For more than two decades, every time I picked up a shoe to shine, every time I wrung out the mop to clean up somebody else's mess or hurried to answer the ringing of the bell as I was summoned to a passenger's compartment, or each time I offered a tray of drinks to travelers, I was getting another lesson in the school of hard knocks. Today I tell people that I finally graduated from that school in 1952, after twenty-two years on the railway. I started at eighty dollars a month, and by the time I left I was making $150 a month.

To get started in my new job, I made trips to Ottawa and Sudbury with an experienced porter guiding me through the paces. My third trip was to Vancouver. It took four nights to travel from Toronto to Vancouver, and at one point we ran off the track – luckily no one was hurt. When we came into Vancouver on May 25, 1930,

I was officially a full-fledged porter. Over the course of twenty-two years I would make more than 250 trips to Vancouver and hundreds more to Ottawa, Montreal, Winnipeg, and Chicago. On an average trip from Toronto to Vancouver, we would leave on Thursday night at about nine o'clock and would arrive in Vancouver at nine o'clock a.m. on Monday.

John Cooper

Ray Lewis: athlete, railway porter, businessman, and Order of Canada recipient.

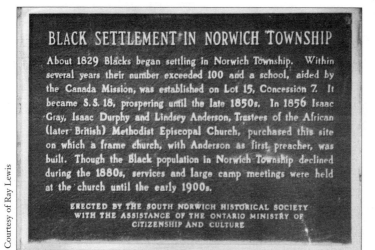

BLACK SETTLEMENT IN NORWICH TOWNSHIP

About 1829 Blacks began settling in Norwich Township. Within several years their number exceeded 100 and a school, aided by the Canada Mission, was established on Lot 15, Concession 7. It became S.S. 18, prospering until the late 1850s. In 1856 Isaac Gray, Isaac Durphy and Lindsey Anderson, Trustees of the African (later British) Methodist Episcopal Church, purchased this site on which a frame church, with Anderson as first preacher, was built. Though the Black population in Norwich Township declined during the 1880s, services and large camp meetings were held at the church until the early 1900s.

ERECTED BY THE SOUTH NORWICH HISTORICAL SOCIETY WITH THE ASSISTANCE OF THE ONTARIO MINISTRY OF CITIZENSHIP AND CULTURE

Isaac Gray, Ray Lewis' paternal great-grandfather, came from the U.S. in 1855 and settled in Otterville, Ontario.

Ray Lewis' ancestors, including Isaac Gray, whose gravesite is pictured here, made significant contributions to Canada's early African-Canadian community.

The Lewis Family, circa World War I: in front, Howard, Emma and Ray; in back, Marjorie, Cornelius, and Victor.

Ray and his brother Howard (left) had lots of fun growing up on Clyde Street in Hamilton, and sports figured highly in their activities every day. They both became competitive runners, but Howard eventually gave up the sport.

The Hamilton Central Collegiate yearbook for Xmas 1928 shows the winning track-and-field team sent to Milwaukee, including Ray (second from right, top row).

Representing his school, Ray (far left) was leadoff man on the mile relay team. He ran at some of North America's most important track-and-field events, against the best Canadian and American runners.

Ray at a track meet at Queen's University in Kingston, Ontario, in 1929. In the 1920s, outdoor races were run on rough cinder tracks, like the one Ray is standing on.

By the time Ray finished high school in 1929, he had an impressive collection of trophies, shown here at the house at 30 Clyde Street. Decades later, Ray would donate all his trophies to Collingwood's Black History and Cultural Museum in Sheffield Park.

Ray Lewis poses in his Canadian team suit – a red blazer with white trim and white flannel pants – at the 1932 Olympic Games in Los Angeles, California.

As a member of the Canadian team at the British Empire Games (now the Commonwealth Games) in 1934, Ray traveled to London, England, in style aboard the *Duchess of York*, one of the many ships in the Canadian Pacific fleet.

The Hamilton Sports Wall of Fame in Copps Coliseum was created by *Hamilton Spectator* editor Jerry Ormond in 1988 to honor Hamilton's top athletes and sports figures. In 1996, Ray was awarded a place on the Hamilton Sports Wall of Fame. "Ray Lewis ran and ran and kept running, and soon joined the elite in the world of track and field."

Ray was a guest of honor at the 2001 Canadian Track and Field Championships in Alberta. He received a standing ovation for his contribution to Canadian sports.

Julien Dupuis, courtesy of Rideau Hall

In February 2001, Ray Lewis received the Order of Canada, Canada's greatest recognition for lifetime achievement. Here, Governor General Adrienne Clarkson presents Ray with the Order of Canada pin.

Courtesy of Ray Lewis and Rideau Hall

After receiving the Order of Canada, Ray and his wife Vivienne were guests at a reception at Rideau Hall, residence of the Governor General of Canada.

CHAPTER 9

TRAINING FOR THE OLYMPICS

*For the next two years, I worked hard and continued
my running, for I was still only twenty years old. I
knew that I was still a standout athlete. I was confident
that I could make the Canadian Olympic team that
would head for Los Angeles in 1932. The competitive
fire still burned inside me. The memory of the racism
of Captain Cornelius and Robert Hunter was fresh in
my mind. I determined that I would prove to them and
to myself that I could be a world-class athlete.*

Working on the railway meant long trips and many days
away from home and family. It meant breaking up my
regular training schedule. The positive side was that it
was a steady job. For many porters, the job gave them a
chance to continue their schooling and to send their kids
to school too. Many porters and their children went on to
attend university and became doctors, lawyers, dentists,
business owners, and politicians. Famous Canadians like
musician Oscar Peterson and Juanita Westmoreland

Traore, the Dean of Law at the University of Windsor, had porters for fathers. The porter job also created civil rights leaders. Porters like Stanley Grizzle would lead the Canadian civil rights movement that would grow in the 1940s and 1950s. So in many ways, while the job reinforced the servant stereotype, it also gave blacks opportunities for education and better jobs. For me, the porter job offered access to many different kinds of people and a host of ideas. Porters, traveling back and forth across the country, became the "ambassadors of the railway" and were leaders in the black community.

Of course, being a black man in a white world meant being stereotyped. Some people believed that rubbing a black man's head would bring them good luck. One time I was helping passengers get on board a train in Winnipeg when a member of Canada's national lacrosse team approached me. He was on his way to a championship game and wanted to rub my head for luck.

I was angry to be treated in such a way. You can only imagine what it must be like to be isolated and treated as if you're less than human, like nothing more than a good luck charm. Despite the fact that he had a crowd of fans surrounding him, who might have turned on me, I pushed his hand away, looked him in the eye, and told him to leave me alone.

The crowd stared in shock and disbelief. They couldn't believe that I would speak that way, not only to a white man, but to a famous athlete as well. And the lacrosse player? He just shrugged and got on the train. I don't think he realized how mean, demoralizing, and hurtful his words were to me. Or maybe he did.

Things weren't always that bad, and the job had its humorous moments. For instance, during an overnight trip to Ottawa, we made a special early-morning stop in Arnprior, a town west of Ottawa. We were there to drop off the premier of Ontario, G. Howard Ferguson, who was on his way to a big announcement. Dawn was just breaking on the eastern horizon, a wash of blues and pinks with just a few stray clouds in the sky, and the train was smoothly chugging down the tracks when I heard the furious ringing of the bell from the Premier's quarters. I rushed into his quarters. There I found the Premier, a strongly built, dignified man, in his pajamas, fumbling about in the covers of his bed. His voice came out as a series of hisses and whistles.

"Ray, I've lost my false teeth," he mumbled. *It wouldn't do to have the premier of the province appearing at a public event without his teeth*, I thought to myself. We ransacked his quarters and finally found the dentures. With his teeth in place, a smile on his face, and his dignity intact, Premier Ferguson disembarked on time.

Passengers on CPR trains enjoyed much comfort during their trips across the country. Porters who had to stay overnight between trips, or "runs" as they were called, stayed in porters' quarters, which were usually owned and operated by the CPR, or we would find our own accommodations, sometimes in a hotel. Porters' quarters were rooming houses – large, square-framed homes whose rooms had been converted into separate apartments, with bunk beds and a few chairs and tables. These quarters could be noisy at night, as porters would get into card games or talk about their jobs, often into the early hours of the morning. If I had the money for a hotel, about fifteen dollars, I would find a clean, well-kept hotel that would accept black people (many wouldn't) and get a good night's sleep.

Porters depended on tips to survive, and we would look to make about 25 cents per night per passenger. When I began working for the CPR, up to 70 percent of black families in Canada were supported in some way by the railway – that's how important it was to our community. If you traveled to Winnipeg, Calgary, Vancouver, or Montreal, you knew where the black families lived and you could meet people in each city who might give you a room if you needed one. The porters were a close-knit group and provided a link that connected the black community across Canada.

In Vancouver, I sometimes stayed with an older woman, Mrs. Pope, whose son was also a porter. She would rent a room to me for two dollars a night. I would arrive at Mrs. Pope's home about noon on Monday, get a few hours of sleep, get up, take a shower, go out and do some running. Later on, I would get cleaned up, get into a suit, and go out to the theater.

Long before television became a household item, theaters didn't feature just movies – they had live entertainment too. You could get into a theater for 75 cents

and see a play or listen to music. You could sit back in a
soft chair covered in red velveteen, and watch as the
house lights were turned down low and the curtain was
drawn back to reveal bright instruments, shining in the
spotlight, and a stage full of dedicated musicians doing
what they loved the most – performing before an appre-
ciative crowd. I would go to listen to jazz musicians like
Lionel Hampton and Illinois Jacquet.

Afterwards, I would get a meal for about 50 cents.
In some areas of Vancouver's downtown there were
restaurants that refused to serve blacks – waiters
might just ignore you, hoping you would leave, or
they could just say up front, "We don't serve you."
In Vancouver's Chinatown it was different – I could
always get a seat and enjoy an all-you-can-eat buffet
for only two dollars.

While black people might be treated with disrespect
on occasion in Vancouver, the white population showed a
lot of racism towards Japanese-Canadians, who were
treated very poorly, especially in the years leading up to
World War II. And in other cities, particularly in the
U.S., the color bar, the invisible social line that separated
blacks from whites, could be sensed strongly. Still, in
some American cities, where the black population was
much bigger than in Canadian towns, you could feel
more comfortable.

One of my favorite cities was Chicago, where I would
go to two shows a day. In Chicago's downtown, there were
always stage orchestras playing in the theaters. You could

go into a theater for the afternoon show, stay for a couple of hours, then come out, cross the street, and catch the five o'clock show at another theater. When the show finished, it would be time to head back to the railroad and get ready for the overnight run.

My porter's job continued to absorb my time and energy. I would get only about three hours of sleep a night, because most of my time was taken up looking after the passengers. But I still found time to train for competitions. In Vancouver, for instance, I would begin a layover – the three days off before the train headed east again – with a shower and a nap. Then I would get into my running gear and head out to local parks like Brockton Point or Hastings Park for a light workout of about two hours before going on to other activities. In Ottawa, I would arrive in the morning after being up all night, and I would sleep three or four hours. I would then head out to train on the cinder path that stretched out alongside the Rideau Canal, in the shadow of Canada's Parliament Buildings. At home in Hamilton, I would continue my daily workouts at local parks or, during the winter, at the Armouries.

And I would work out wherever the train stopped. Occasionally we would stop on the prairies. The wind whistled past the train and tall spires of grain waved in the light breeze. The sky was a blue like I've never seen before or since, bluer than a robin's egg, with just a few stray cirrus clouds high above. I would check with the conductor and, if we had an hour or so to wait, I would get into my training gear, lace up my running shoes, and have a workout.

I ran smoothly alongside the train, pounding out my paces in the dirt path beside the track, watching out for ruts and listening to nothing but my steady breathing and the soft sound of my feet coming down on the earth. I glanced at my shadow as I ran alongside the track to make sure my posture was correct. The steel rails threw shadows across the timbers of the track, making changing geometric patterns as I ran. The prairies were so even and smooth, I could easily see where the sky met the earth, far away in the distance. When you're a runner on the prairies, you almost feel like you can run forever. Many a farmer would pause in his work to watch me, and – from North Dakota to Minnesota, Saskatchewan to Alberta, B.C. to Northern Ontario – whenever the train stopped and I could manage it, I would be running alongside the rails. After an hour, the train's whistle blew, calling me back. It was back into my porter's uniform and back to work, looking after the passengers. My Olympic dreams were put back into storage, too.

On some trips across the country we would carry no passengers. It was called "deadheading," and it was a way of moving empty rail cars across the country. On these runs, our main job was to ensure that hobos didn't climb on board for a free ride. On some trains you could have as many as twenty hobos hoisting themselves up ladders when the train was stopped.

A common sight as they criss-crossed the country looking for work, hobos were dressed in blue jeans and work boots, with battered hats and checked shirts, often with a red neckerchief completing the look. The railway police, special constables hired by the CPR, would be busy trying to haul these itinerant workers, mostly men, who traveled all over North America, off the trains. For the most part, the hobos didn't do anyone any harm – they were just trying to survive the Depression like everyone else.

While working on the CPR, I met a lot of other athletes and former athletes. Despite the racist attitudes of the time, athletes often enjoyed friendships that went beyond the color line. It was like an invisible force that connected us. We knew what it was like to train hard for competition. We knew the demands that sports made on our bodies and our minds. Although society didn't see it the same way, there was good-natured equality that existed between us, whether black or white.

Meeting leading sports figures opened a few doors for me – like coach Jack Adams of the Detroit Red Wings obtaining permission for me to work out at the Olympia sports complex when I was in Detroit. The great sprinter Ralph Metcalfe got me into Soldiers Field in Chicago, and in Montreal, Tommy Gorman of the Montreal Canadiens enabled me to train at the Forum.

In fact, when the Detroit Red Wings were traveling from city to city by train, I would often be serving them. I

did the same for the Chicago Blackhawks and the
Toronto Maple Leafs. These hockey players, many of
whom would go on to become stars of their era, always
treated me with respect. On a trip with the Toronto
Maple Leafs, when they were returning from playing the
Canadiens, Leafs star Francis Michael "King" Clancy,
who knew about my running career, asked me if I would
be running in a meet in Hamilton the next night.

"I'll be running in the 1000-yard event," I told him. It
was late at night and I knew I would only get two or three
hours of rest before we pulled into Toronto.

"You must be tired," the small but feisty Leafs
defenseman replied. "How are you going to be ready for
it if you don't get some rest?"

"I'll manage," was my reply. But I knew I'd be tired.

Clancy gave me a wink and offered me his own bunk.
"You flake out in my bed and I'll listen for the bell. Just
about everybody's asleep on this train already! You know
there's not going to be a lot happening at this time of
night. But if there is, don't worry, I'll take care of things."

So I stretched out in Clancy's bunk and got a few
hours of rest while this great hockey player, the heart and
soul and spiritual leader of the Maple Leafs, donned his
imaginary porter's cap. And true to his words, nobody
rang the bell. The next day I won the race, thanks at least
in small part to being well rested, courtesy of King Clancy.

CHAPTER 10

I JOIN CANADA'S OLYMPIC TEAM

◆

*While I didn't have an opportunity to run races out-
doors in 1930 or 1931, I did run at indoor meets and
took part in some interesting competitions. I won some,
and in others I came in second or third.*

By the spring of 1932, I felt I was ready to try for Canada's
Olympic team. There was a real sense of excitement
about how Canada might do at the Summer Games in
Los Angeles, California, and a feeling that Canadian
athletes were beginning to really distinguish themselves
among the world's top athletes. Earlier in the year, at the
Winter Games in Lake Placid, New York, the Canadian
team had gone home with seven medals.

I look back on my attitude and I know that, when I
ran, I wasn't in it for the medals. I was there to establish a
personal best for myself. My goal was to do better than I
had ever done before. And if it meant a medal-winning
performance, then so be it. But I wasn't looking for glory

– only to prove that a black Canadian could find a place on a Canadian Olympic team.

The Canadian trials for the Summer Games were held in my hometown, at Hamilton's Civic Stadium. It was a familiar place for me, and being in front of a supportive crowd that knew my accomplishments helped me stay relaxed and ready. I was able to get a month's leave of absence from my job to attend the trials.

And after a good showing at the trials, I made the team – the first Canadian-born black man on a Canadian track-and-field team. It meant, of course, that I would be running under the direction of Captain Cornelius, my old high-school coach. His attitude towards blacks hadn't changed, so I just buckled down and ran as well as I could.

Cap Cornelius and M.M. Robinson were at that time two of Canada's best-known sports figures, and they were always at odds with each other over coaching – especially over the Olympic track-and-field team. As a result of a dispute, Robinson brought in a well-known coach named Nick Bawlf, who had played on winning football and lacrosse teams, and was considered by many as a coach who could really motivate his runners. He was aggressive, and he was used to getting results by intimidating people and making them feel that they weren't up to his standards of performance. And like Cornelius, Bawlf held some very negative opinions of black athletes, something that would come out during training.

By the late spring, Canada's track-and-field team had been chosen and we were preparing for Los Angeles. We were working out in June temperatures that were reaching 35° Celsius. I recall a workout at the Civic Stadium on a scorching hot day and hearing Bawlf calling to me. "Lewis, get over here!" he yelled. "I want to talk to you." I jogged up to him, dripping sweat.

"Lewis!" he yelled as I approached. "What have you done today?"

"I just finished doing 660 yards at three-quarter speed," I said. That was the standard workout for that part of our training.

"That's not enough, Lewis," he said. "You need to do more." Then he glared at me with the same look of hatred I had seen before in the eyes of white people. "You're pretty lazy, Lewis."

I was angry. The same feelings I'd had with Cap and with Robert Hunter welled up in me. To many white people, if blacks weren't servants or clowns, they were lazy.

"How do you think I made the team if I'm lazy?" I asked. I walked away without waiting for a reply. I went over to the manager of the men's team, Bobby Kerr.

I figured that if anyone would understand my position it would be Bobby Kerr. Born in Ireland, he had lived in Hamilton for many years. He had brought Canada a gold in the 200-meter sprint and a bronze in the 100 meters from the 1908 Olympics in London, England. For fifteen years, he held the title of World's Greatest Sprinter. So he was more than qualified to deal with situations between athletes and their coaches.

"Bobby, I don't have to go to California," I said to him. "It doesn't mean anything to me to go to California. But I made the team. I am representing Canada. Tell Nick to get off my back, or I won't be going to California. He just told me I'm lazy – and he doesn't even know me!"

Bobby Kerr could hear the pain in my voice and spoke to Bawlf. After that, Bawlf never said another word to me, neither at training nor during the entire Olympic Games.

I sure didn't need somebody like Nick Bawlf to tell me how to run or how hard to train. I knew what to do to prepare for a race. And when the race came, I knew how to get ready for it. I was certainly familiar with my specialty, the 400-meter run. The 400 meters required that runners cover a full lap of the track, and was the longest race for which runners had to stay in their own lane the entire time. This meant a staggered start for runners, so that they were not lined up side-by-side at the start.

I loved the feel of getting ready for a race. I knew how to get settled into my blocks, my toes digging into the cinder or crushed peat of the track. I would settle my feet in, heels just above the ground, with my arms almost straight out, hands just behind the starting line and shoulders high. I would get ready and breathe in when I heard the command "Set!" that let us know the gun was about to go off to start the race. I would shift my hips up and move my weight forward until my weight was balanced on my fingertips.

On the sound of the gun, I drove hard out of the blocks. My arms were pumping and my strides were fast. I would race out of the blocks quickly, with a long and strong stride. I was good at getting a fast start and would often be the first one out of the blocks.

I would hold my head up and look straight ahead. And I would relax, even though my body was working hard. As a runner, it's important that you stay calm and that your shoulders and arms stay relaxed; otherwise, your body will burn up energy too quickly. At the same time, you must focus on making the most of your leg movement. On the bends of the track, you want to stick to the inside of your lane and run at a pace slightly slower than top speed. Then, when you're in the open and in the final straight length of track, you can use your energy reserves to bring you home.

When we trained for relay racing, we focused on specific techniques for passing the baton, in addition to running. You need to position yourself on the track properly in order to hand off and receive the baton in the right way. In relay races I was usually the leadoff runner, mainly because of my fast starts and my ability to run well on the bends of the track. The incoming runner, the one holding the baton, and the outgoing runner who receives the baton must be running at the same speed when the baton is handed over. The baton is passed from the left hand of the incoming runner to the right hand of the outgoing runner. And when you do it right, it's a great process that combines good athletics and great concentration.

CHAPTER 11

LOS ANGELES AND THE OLYMPIC GAMES

◈

When the big day came to travel to the 10th Olympic
Games in Los Angeles, California, I joined my team at
Toronto's Union Station to board the train, which was
dubbed The Olympic Special. The date was July 21,
1932, and we hauled our modest suitcases to the
platform; for clothing and essentials, we packed lightly,
but with dreams of Olympic glory, those cases were
brimming almost to bursting.

As for me, I was glad to be a passenger, rather than a
porter, on that Olympic train. It was nice to hang up
my hat and just enjoy the ride for a change. My family
saw me off. There were a few tears, lots of hugs, and a
promise to send a postcard or two. And I knew they
would follow my progress in the newspaper.

On the four-day trip, we traveled with the English
track team, the Polish water polo team, and various
athletes from South Africa, Belgium, and Hungary. When
we made a stop in Chicago, we were given a VIP tour of

the famous Windy City. During the whole trip, we were treated with dignity and respect. We truly (and for some of us, for the first time) felt like world-class athletes.

The economic times in Los Angeles continued to be difficult. Times were indeed tough all over – members of the Brazilian Olympic team, for instance, brought bags of coffee with them to sell as they traveled, even on the streets of Los Angeles, to raise money for their trip. Yet the city of Los Angeles was well prepared for the Games. The Olympic Stadium, previously called the Los Angeles Coliseum, was located on a seventeen-acre site (almost 8 hectares). It was built in the early 1920s, and additional work in preparation for the games was done in 1930 – especially creating more seating, from 75,000 seats to 105,000. Built along the lines of an ancient Roman amphitheater, the Coliseum would, many years later, host the 1984 Olympics in addition to these 1932 Games.

Above the entrance to the stadium's track area were the words of France's Baron Pierre de Coubertin: "The important thing in the Olympic Games is not winning but taking part. The essential thing in life is not conquering but fighting well."

De Coubertin is often called the Father of the modern Olympic Games. He began the process of bringing back the Olympics in 1892. For more than 1500 years, the Olympic Games, originally held in Athens, Greece, had been dormant. No contests were held and no athletes displayed their skills and abilities before large crowds. De Coubertin decided to resurrect the Games. In 1896

the first modern Olympic Games were held, and they
continued every four years from then.

The Olympics were, and still are, about personal bests.
Even though athletes represent their home countries, de
Coubertin's ideal was that, through competition, Olympic
athletes show how well they can do as individuals.

I took that ideal, and the Baron's own words, to heart.
Although I was representing my country and I was proud
of it, I also wanted to prove to myself that I could compete
with the best. I felt I had already lived by the Baron's
words. I had certainly fought well, especially in standing
up for myself in the face of hatred. When I made the
Olympic track-and-field team, I was the first Canadian-
born black man on it, and I got to Los Angeles myself – no
porter's cap, no long hours of picking up after others, no
long and lonely nights traveling across the country.

The Los Angeles Coliseum cost $2 million to build. The
running track was made of crushed peat. Crushed peat
was a better surface than cinder for many runners, and
one that improved the times in many events. Tickets to
each event cost between one and three dollars, and these
Games were the first to introduce the three-level winners
podium that has become so common since. Altogether,
1400 athletes (including 127 women) from thirty-seven
countries competed. More than 700 reporters from
newspapers and magazines worldwide would attend.

A total of thirty-three Olympic records and sixteen
world records were broken at the 1932 Olympic Games,

and it was significant for having the very first Olympic Village, built at a cost of $400,000. The Village was designed to keep costs down by allowing athletes to live and train together at only two dollars per athlete per day. It was so popular at the 1932 Games that it became a fixture at every Olympic Games since then. That first Olympic Village was for men only – the 127 female athletes stayed at the Chapman Park Hotel.

The Olympic Village was a sight like no other. It was big – 325 acres (130 hectares) – and was located ten minutes from the stadium in the Baldwin Hills. It had many kilometers of pathways and roads that wound around 500 hacienda-style cottages, painted white and pink, and more than 30,000 flowering plants. Each cottage housed four athletes and had conveniences that many of us had never seen before, like hot showers, reading tables, and telephones, as well as specially woven Olympic towels. It had a post office, hospital, library, and barbershop. Around the outside of the fence that enclosed the Village, vaqueros, the Southwest's cowboys, patrolled on horseback.

All the athletes were able to choose food from special menus, with specialties from each competing country that reflected their national foods. There were forty-two kitchens, and the Games' twenty-three chefs, sixteen assistant chefs, and 130 kitchen helpers served more than 100,000 meals. What a treat for me, who was used to eating whatever leftovers might be in the dining car on the CPR!

The accommodations were comfortable and true to
the ideal. We got to know each other, and differences
between people – racial, cultural, and national – began to
melt away. We became what the organizers had intended
– a brotherhood of international athletes, training
together and competing together.

The opening ceremonies took place on a blazing hot
July 30. It was a wonderful experience for the Canadian
team. In the stands, more than 100,000 spectators stood
and cheered as we entered the stadium. We were told that
more than 30,000 of those spectators were Canadians. We
paraded past the stands wearing red blazers with white
trim, with white flannel pants for the men and white
skirts for the women. And we received a standing ovation.

The vice president of the United States, Charles
Curtis, opened the Olympic Games with the announcement: "I proclaim open the Olympic Games of Los
Angeles, celebrating the 10th Olympiad of the modern
era." Curtis pushed a button to light the Olympic Torch,
and more than 2000 rock doves were released to celebrate
the opening.

To say I was excited to be there would be an under-
statement. It was the realization of my dream that began
the first time I ran down Clyde Street, my only competition the neighborhood kids and my sheer will to win.
Now, I had a chance to compete against the world's best
athletes, to live with them and to learn from them.

In Los Angeles I got to know some famous people.
One day I put on my training gear and headed out for a

run. There, on a street corner, stretching to prepare for
his training run, was the great Italian athlete Luigi Beccali.
At these Olympics, he would go on to set a new Olympic
record of 3 minutes, 51.2 seconds in the 1500-meter run.
But here he was, getting ready to train. I smiled at him
and nodded. Together, we ran through the streets of Los
Angeles, getting ready for our events. It was a silent
training partnership, of course, for neither one of us
spoke the other's language. But we trained together for
four days. I was saddened later on to see that this great
athlete would, while standing on the winners podium,
raise his hand in the fascist salute, a sign of hatred that
during World War II would become a terrible symbol of
anti-Semitism, oppression, and death.

This being Los Angeles, we athletes met our share of
celebrities, like Douglas Fairbanks, Marlene Dietrich,
Clara Bow, Mary Pickford, Charlie Chaplin, Gary Cooper,
Cary Grant, Bing Crosby, and the Marx Brothers. It was
considered very trendy for the celebrities to walk around
and collect autographs from the foreign teams – and we
definitely got our share of autographs from them.

When I wasn't training under the critical and watch-
ful eye of Cap Cornelius, I hung out with the other
members of the Canadian team, especially with my relay
teammates: Alex Wilson, Jimmy Ball, and Phil Edwards.
And there was Percy Williams, the leader of our team,
who later had to pull out because of a thigh injury.

Percy Williams came by the leadership role naturally:
he had won gold at the 1928 Olympics in the 100 meters

(at 10.8 seconds) and the 200 meters, and would be voted Canada's Greatest Track Athlete of the first half of the 20th century.

Alex Wilson would go on to win a bronze in the individual 400-meter event, a bronze in our 4 x 400-meter relay, and a silver in the 800 meters at those 1932 Olympics.

Jimmy Ball, who was originally from Manitoba, was a standout at the 1928 Olympics, where he won a silver medal in the 400 meters.

Phil Edwards was also an outstanding Canadian athlete. He had competed in the 1928 Olympic Games (winning a bronze medal in the 4 x 400-meter relay). At the 1932 Olympics he would come third in the 1500-meter event that Beccali won, and win bronze in the 800 meters, along with our team bronze in the 4 x 400-meter relay. He would go on to win another bronze in the 800-meter race at the 1936 Olympics. Born in Georgetown, Guyana (at the time known as British Guiana), Phil was a great runner who became a doctor and an expert in tropical diseases. He was a fast starter who could set a grueling pace for other runners.

Phil and I were the only black athletes on the Canadian team out of a total contingent of 160. The *Hamilton Spectator* of August 9, 1932, carried a photograph of Beccali breaking the tape in the 1500, with Edwards trailing behind. Though his racial background was clearly evident in the photograph, the photo's caption refers to Phil as the "coloured boy from Canada."

I would be out training or at the track and occasionally watch the women athletes as they worked hard, not only to get ready for their races, but also to simply establish a place for women in the Olympic Games. The fact that women even competed at those Olympic Games was significant, for in 1931 the International Olympic Committee had debated the possible elimination of women's events.

In particular, my attention was drawn to a strongly built young woman who was generating a great deal of excitement from competitors and from the press. It was Mildred "Babe" Didrikson, one of many heroes this Olympics would create, one who would be honored for her athletic feats for many years to come. She was strong and tough and walked with confidence around the field. We thought of her as the "goddess of the Games," she attracted so much attention. Babe set several records in her events, capturing gold in the 80-meter hurdles and javelin throw, and a silver medal in the high jump. The involvement and popularity of star athletes like Didrikson soon made female athletics a permanent part of the Olympic Games.

Elsewhere on the track was a smiling and confident man, the lesser-known but no less heroic Eddie Tolan, who in May 1929 became the first man to record 9.5 seconds over 100 yards.

What a comparison! Didrikson, white and female, was dubbed the Texas Tornado and the Terrific Tomboy by star-struck reporters, and would go on to become a top professional golfer; she won twelve major tournaments, including three U.S. Opens. Her life was captured in books and in movies. Tolan, by contrast, was a black runner from Denver, Colorado. He was a University of Michigan graduate and the 1931 National Collegiate champion in the 220 yards. He also won four Amateur Athletic Union (AAU) sprint titles.

With his thick-framed glasses taped to his head to hold them in place, Tolan might have looked a bit nerdy by today's standards. But he was a powerhouse, 5 feet, 7 inches in height, with a strong build and an explosive start. In competition, he ran the 100 meters in 10.3 seconds, matching the world record, to take the gold. He also won gold in the 200 meters with a run of 21.1 seconds, setting an Olympic record. Known as the Midnight Express, Tolan was the first black athlete to win two Olympic gold medals. Over his career, he won 300 races and lost only seven.

After the Olympics, Eddie worked as a performer in the live theater known as vaudeville. Later in his life he taught school. When he died in 1967, he was virtually unknown by mainstream society – and yet his athletic excellence had secured him an important place among black athletes.

In the 1930s, the rule of thumb for the black athlete was simple: you had to be not one hundred, but *1000 percent better* than white athletes if you were going to compete. You had to be stronger, faster, and more mature. You had to show greater respect for the coach than your white teammates did. And you had to be able to speak well with sportswriters or the general public. Many white athletes, by contrast, were grandstanding and sometimes arrogant. A black athlete had to be calm and confident but never pushy. Anything less than that and you could forget about being a competitive athlete.

There were other black athletes at the Olympics too: Ralph Metcalfe, who had beaten Eddie Tolan in the trials, was a standout at the 1936 Berlin Olympics and much later became a U.S. Congressman. There was long jumper Ed Gordon and high jumper Cornelius Johnson, who also distinguished himself at the Berlin Olympics, and two African-American female sprinters, Tidye Pickett and Louise Stokes. While Pickett and Stokes were great athletes, they were never allowed to compete.

On a warm August day, I ran in the elimination rounds of the individual 400-meter run, placing second in Heat 6 of the first round with a time of 50.7 seconds, and placing fifth in Heat 3 of the second round with a time of 49.1 seconds; it was good, but it wasn't enough to send me to the final.

The 4 x 400 meter-relay was more satisfying for me. In Heat 2 of round one, our team placed third, with a time of 3 minutes, 21.8 seconds. With that time in mind, we set ourselves focusing on the final. We were ready. We paced alongside the track, each of us deeply immersed in thought. My thoughts were on winning, on doing well.

I thought of my parents back in Hamilton. I thought of my time on the trains and those long days and nights of travel and work. I wanted more than anything to do well and to bring home a medal.

In the final, I was chosen to run the first leg because I had the speed to break open quickly. Our team was confident that if we got the lead, we could hold on to it for the duration. It was a bright sunny day and track conditions were good. We knew that the crushed peat track had improved the finishing times, and we were counting on it working in our favor. There was a slight breeze, but nothing that would either help or hinder the runners. We knew, too, that our competition was tough. The American team – Ivan Fuqua, Ed Ablowich, Karl Warner, and Bill Carr – was formidable.

I always had a high degree of excitement when I raced, but before this final run my adrenaline was pumping. I took some deep breaths and kept my perspective. As a runner, you always need to maintain your focus. I dug my feet into the holes in the track, focused on the far end of the track, and waited for the gun to go off.

With the 4 x 400-meter race, you have to really be a thinker and pace yourself. The gun went off and I raced down the track, pacing myself at first, and then increasing my speed into the final stretch. I could hear the footfalls of the other competitors and the sound of breathing, even though the sounds were beginning to be drowned out by the crowd. I could see Jimmy Ball starting to run into the

20-meter handover zone, his hand outstretched to receive the baton, a look of concentration on his face. I passed the baton to him and he raced down the track, handing off to Phil Edwards. Phil took off, setting a hard, fast pace, and then passed the baton to Alex Wilson. Wilson, a fleet and nimble runner, streamed down the lane the way white water churns down a riverbed. So balanced and smooth an athlete was he that his legs drove like pistons into the track, driving him forward to the finish line, just steps behind the American runner. The finish was close, so close that all three top teams broke the old Olympic record in the event. We came within 4.6 seconds of the winners, taking the bronze with a time of 3 minutes, 12.8 seconds, behind a winning U.S. team that set a world record with 3 minutes, 8.2 seconds. Great Britain came second in a time of 3 minutes, 11.2 seconds.

After Alex Wilson charged over the finish line, we gathered around him. He looked up at the finishing times and exclaimed, "Hey! Look, we broke the record too!" It was a great moment for us all.

Carr, Fuqua, Ablowich, and Warner were ecstatic as they headed for the medal podium. But we were proud too, as the crowd cheered and the flashbulbs of the newspaper photographers popped all around us. It was a great Olympic year for Canada; we won a total of fifteen medals at that Summer Olympic Games.

The closing ceremonies were just as extravagant and beautiful as the opening ceremonies. The 105,000 spectators in the stadium, filling it to capacity, sang along with the contingent of 1000 singers, "Aloha, Farewell Until We Meet Again."

Some of those athletes I *would* meet again, in competition over the next few years. For many of them, though, this Olympics was their swan song.

When we prepared to return from the Games, several of us – including my 4 x 400-meter teammates, Lefty Gwynn, who won a gold in boxing, high jumper Jack Portland, who later played professional hockey, long jumper Lenny Hutton, and I – were each handed an envelope by the organizers of the Canadian team. Inside was a rail ticket home, with the Los Angeles-to-Chicago portion designated as an upper berth, and twenty-five dollars in cash.

You couldn't travel in better style than that. But what did we do? Most of us needed the money, so we sold those precious upper berths to other passengers. We sat in the coach section and enjoyed the trip home. We were happy just to have had an opportunity to compete.

I was especially pleased with my performance. I became one of only three male Hamiltonians to win an Olympic track medal, joining Billy Sherring (1906) and Bobby Kerr (1908).

But when I arrived home, I made the long jump back from world-class Olympian to CPR porter.

CHAPTER 12

BACK ON THE CPR

◆

*I returned from the Olympics to a warm welcome from
my family. We gathered at our home on Clyde Street
and invited some friends over to celebrate.*

I had reason to celebrate everything but my job. Despite
having represented Canada honorably, there were no
good job prospects for me. Even though the Depression
was still on, I watched as other athletes, all white, got jobs.

After the Olympics, Phil Edwards went off to finish
his training as a doctor. But generally speaking, there
were no decent jobs for black men. I was told that over
and over again as I knocked on the doors of many businesses. One man offered me a job as an elevator operator,
riding up and down in an elevator all day and opening the
door for passengers. Another said I couldn't work at his
office because his customers wouldn't deal with him if he
had a black man on staff.

So I put the uniform of the porter – and all the attitudes of other people that came with it – back on.

In order to make a decent living as a porter, I had to
learn how to turn off my anger and put on an artificial

smile. I learned how to offer a crisp, "Good morning sir!"
or "Good morning, ma'am, did you have a good night?"
Most white passengers, in fact, wanted to be seen being
nice to porters, in a condescending way of course. We
were treated much like the characters we saw in the
movies, as if we were subservient and enjoyed serving
white people, as if our lives were made so much better
by the handing out of a 25-cent tip.

It was a world of service. It meant greeting people and
helping them on the train, carrying their luggage, making
their beds, cleaning their toilets, brushing off their clothes,
getting them food, shining their shoes, and helping them
off the train when it arrived at its destination.

It was also a world where I learned to control my
temper. That was a must – for if a passenger said anything
negative about a porter to the porter's supervisor, the
CPR was almost always on the passenger's side. The word
of a white person was considered over that of a black man
almost every time. We earned demerit points if there
were complaints. You could receive 30 points for being
rude to a passenger. At 60 points you were automatically
fired. So it's no surprise that porters were always polite,
even in the face of obnoxious or racist behavior.

CPR trains, like other rail lines, were famous for
running on time. There were – and still are – lots of
sayings about the timeliness of trains. Most conductors
were so focused on keeping to their schedule that, if a
train was due in the station by 9:15, you could literally set
your watch by it. It also meant that if any time was lost in

waiting for a track to open or because of a mechanical breakdown, without a doubt that train would later be rocketing down the rails at breakneck speed to make up the lost time.

We traveled through all kinds of terrain, from the woods and valleys of northwestern Ontario, past fast-running rivers, through the wide, flat expanse of prairies, all blue sky and fields of yellow grain, to the enormous Rocky Mountains, with wisps of cloud encircling their peaks.

CPR passengers were just as different as the landscape we passed through on our travels. There were those who drank too much alcohol so you had to steer them to their beds. There were others who would make demands of you all the time, ringing the porter's bell constantly, then never even bother to tip you at the end of the run. Some were cheerful and gregarious and would love to share stories with the porters. And others were so quiet, you almost forgot they were there.

You had to be prepared for those with bad tempers, of course. In one incident, a young porter from the southern U.S. was working diligently near me serving passengers. Unfortunately, he got into an argument with a grumpy old man, who struck the porter with his cane. The young man came to me with tears in his eyes. He was angry and, because the CPR did nothing to reprimand the old man, ended up quitting.

"I'm going back to the South," he said. "At least *down there* I know where I stand." Indeed, in the southern U.S.

there were actual laws segregating blacks from whites. Blacks couldn't use some washrooms designated as "whites only." They couldn't eat in some restaurants and couldn't drink from "whites only" water fountains – the list was almost endless. He came north, believing there was more tolerance in Canada. How wrong he was about that!

We also had our share of cheapskates! On one trip, a very proper British businessman traveled in a double compartment from Vancouver to Toronto. In every way, he appeared to be the perfect traveler: neat, well mannered, and possessing a clean, clipped British accent. I attended to his every need during the trip. At the end of the run he gave me a one-dollar tip. It was about one-tenth of what he should have tipped for the space he took and the service he received. That was always a disheartening experience – to work hard and give the best service possible, only to be given a terrible tip. It made a lot of porters angry. For me, I just buried the anger and got on with serving the next passengers, hoping they might be more generous.

There were some generous passengers, like the owner of a major league baseball team who would give me a ten-dollar tip at the start of the trip to look after his needs. And a senior executive with the automobile maker General Motors was equally generous.

But racist attitudes were always present on the rails. On one run a passenger said to me "Do you like watermelon, *boy?*" He emphasized the last word. "Boy" was often used in reference to black men, who were definitely not boys, when some white people wanted to assert their social position. This passenger thought all black people liked watermelon. It was a stereotype that had been around a long time. I couldn't say much back to him, because I would get in trouble by talking back. By I could offer an interesting reply.

"Yes sir, we like it fried," I replied, knowing, as he did, that nobody ate watermelon like that. "Fried, all the time, sir." The man knew that behind my calm, cool exterior and matter-of-fact answer, I was making fun of his attitude. But he couldn't say or do anything about it.

Other passengers would call me "George," after the inventor of the railway sleeping car, George Pullman. Porters were called "George's boys" in the late 19th and early 20th centuries and the name stuck. By the time I worked on the CPR, it had been shortened to just "George."

Polite passengers might call me simply "Porter," but for others it was often either "Hey, George," or "Come here, boy!"

We had ways of dealing with that kind of rudeness. One evening I was serving passengers soft drinks, and I had a passenger who nearly "boyed" me to death. I just ignored him. Every time he called, "Hey, boy!" or "Boy!" I would be doing something else. Finally he called out to me, "Excuse me, porter," and I turned and replied, "Oh, did you need something, sir?" It drew the attention of everyone in the rail car. He was clearly embarrassed, ordered a ginger ale and then quickly left.

But serving passengers also meant shining their shoes, and that was a part of the job I really disliked.

I brushed thousands of shoes during my time on the CPR. There were rules for shoe shining. You had to wait until passengers were asleep and quietly remove the shoes, which were left outside the berths. As the train rumbled along the tracks, you took each shoe and, with a piece of chalk, marked the berth number on the sole so that you could return the shoes later. Then you would work for the next couple of hours, in the quiet light of your porter's room, applying shoe polish and buffing the shoes to a shine. When the passengers awoke in the morning, they would find their shoes clean and neatly shined.

A porter's life could be very unpredictable. Even on their days off, porters could find themselves heading out of town on a moment's notice. And that moment's notice could turn into many days of traveling.

Let me give you an example: One night I drew station duty. On station duty you didn't travel on the trains. Your job was to carry a set of diagrams of the inside of the train cars, showing which berths had been bought by passengers, to the conductor. But what should happen when I arrive at the conductor's office? One of the other porters was not going on that run, and so I was quickly put to work in his place. I traveled to Winnipeg on an extra

car that was added to that train, then deadheaded on
an empty train back to Fort William, now the city of
Thunder Bay, Ontario. Here the train picked up members
of the British Medical Association, who were heading out
to Vancouver. We took seven days to get there, stopping
in Winnipeg, Regina, Banff, and Lake Louise. I had two
days off in Vancouver, then got back on the train and was
sent to Chicago. From Chicago, we deadheaded to St.
Paul, Minnesota. We stopped overnight in a little town
outside St. Paul, small enough that I can't remember its
name, only that it had a small main street with a bank,
post office, grocery store, and gas station. It was a pictur-
esque place of pine trees and gentle hills. The air was
crisp and clean. But all the beauty of the place was lost on
me, for I hadn't eaten in almost two days. I really needed
some food – and fast!

There was no food to be found on the train and I had
only four dollars in my pocket. Another porter I was with,
named Jim Wiltshire, had no money at all. The two of us
wandered down the road, probably looking lost so far
from home, and nervous because we were the only black
people in this all-white town. I went to the bank first to
change my Canadian dollars into American money. We
then headed across the street to the grocery store, where
we managed to buy some pork, potatoes, and corn. We
cooked up our little feast in the train kitchen.

The train resumed its trip the next day, heading back
to Vancouver. We came back to St. Paul on another train,
then deadheaded back to Calgary, and finally finished the

trip by deadheading home. When I arrived, tired and
weary, I had been gone six weeks! All on a moment's
notice. But I was also able to pocket $125 in wages for
my time away.

And while the situation wasn't ideal, porters knew
that wherever we went, there were people who were less
fortunate. We could always count on seeing the wayward
travelers, the hobos, during a run. We would pass their
communities, called Hobo Jungles, on the side of the
railway tracks. They were raggedy but clean, and they followed a rule of conduct that was decent and upstanding.
They would congregate around an open fire, over which
hung an iron pot of stew made up of anything the hobos
could scrounge together – a bit of beef, some potatoes,
some carrots. And the hobos looked out for each other.
Many of them had keys to the railway cars and would let
themselves in. When this happened, we porters were
under strict orders to leave them alone and to lock ourselves in the end car. I would often leave little things out
for them, like soap, and many times I would see a hobo
crouched by a stream just a few feet away from his
encampment, giving himself a wash.

There wasn't much work for the hobos, especially
on the prairies. A drought had turned the prairies, from
the American midwest up into Canada, into a dustbowl
from 1930 to 1937. As we traveled across the tracks, we
watched dust devils whirl up across the plains. Dirt blew
through the air like a filthy snowstorm and piled around
farm buildings in huge, dark drifts. I watched over the

years as farm equipment, sitting unused in one place year after year, eventually fell apart.

Things weren't looking too good for many people. For me, the tough times only made me work harder. I still had more to prove, to myself and to those who would hold me back from realizing my potential. The British Empire Games were coming in 1934. I was determined to make the team and represent my country, as I had done at the Olympics.

CHAPTER 13

THE BRITISH EMPIRE GAMES

◈

The British Empire Games were held in London, England, from August 4 to 11, 1934. As M.M. "Bobby" Robinson had envisioned, these games would grow from their humble start in Hamilton in 1930 to provide an opportunity for athletes to compete in an atmosphere of friendship, whether they were from Canada, New Zealand, Jamaica, Australia, Kenya – any country on the map that Great Britain had colonized during the past three centuries.

They were called the British Empire Games until 1950. In 1954, they became the British Empire & Commonwealth Games, then the British Commonwealth Games in 1970. They have been known simply as the Commonwealth Games since 1974.

In the 1934 Games, 500 athletes from 16 countries competed in athletics, boxing, cycling, lawn bowling, swimming, diving, and wrestling. It was also the first year that women's events were featured. The Games' track-and-field events were held at White City Stadium, which was built for the 1908 Olympics. It was called White City because of the color of the buildings constructed on the site for the Great Exhibition, also held there in 1908. The Olympics were held right next door to the Great Exhibition.

British athletes used the White City Stadium for their Olympic training and, in the late 1920s, it was even used as a greyhound track. In 1931 a new running track was built, which was used for the 1934 Games. Used regularly by two-legged and four-legged athletes for the next fifty years, the stadium was torn down in the 1980s. Today, the offices of the British Broadcasting Corporation occupy the site.

We traveled to the Games on the *Duchess of York*, one of a line of transatlantic ships operated by Canadian Pacific, which also ran the trains that I worked on. It could accommodate 1500 passengers, and was big and grand in every way. It had been launched in 1928 and was eventually bombed by the Germans during World War II while transporting troops across the ocean.

We spent ten days crossing the Atlantic Ocean. All of the Canadian athletes were eager to compete and excited about the trip; we literally took over the ship. We were all over it, from bow to stern. We jogged on the deck to stay in shape and enjoyed the camaraderie of being part of the Canadian team. When we arrived, our team stayed in a hotel at the gates of Kensington Garden, near Hyde Park. Kensington Garden is a beautiful place, with pathways, old trees, statues of royalty, and a pond filled with swans. It was peaceful, and the fields of green, marked by old, stately trees, made our stay relaxing.

All of us on the Canadian track-and-field team wanted to try the English food. And while it was good, the portions weren't what we considered Canadian-size. For instance, one of our Canadian team swimmers, George Larson, had ordered an "English steak" at a London restaurant, expecting to get a good-size piece of steak. Like all of us, George had a big appetite. He was a great swimmer whose efforts had resulted in his being named city senior champion in Hamilton. But when the meal arrived, what did he find on his plate but a tiny piece of overcooked beef! "What the heck am I going to do with that?" George asked, looking down at his plate and poking at the steak.

We trained for our events at a track called Shepherd's Bush, which we traveled to via the London Underground, or subway. It was called Shepherd's Bush because at one time, hundreds of years before, shepherds would use the ground as a rest stop on their way to market with their flocks.

At the track, our team worked hard to get ready for the Games. For the 4 x 440-yard race, our team members included Bill Fritz, another fellow Canadian named Scott, who came from Windsor, Ontario, and Joe Addison, a great athlete who would die years later, fighting for Canada in World War II. The weather was excellent and our practices went well.

I faced some tough competition, but our team managers felt that I had a good chance to win the individual 440-yard race. I qualified easily in my first heat, and came up in the final qualifying race against Joe Addison.

I lined up in my lane and, at the sound of the gun, took off fast, establishing an early lead. I was feeling good but, coming into the final stretch, I realized I had been running far too fast. I was getting tired too quickly. Joe passed me. The other runners passed me. I ran out of energy and came last, eliminated from the final.

The winner of the 440 yards was Godfrey Rampling of Great Britain, who ran it in 48 seconds. Rampling was also a member of the 4 x 400-meter relay team that won a silver medal at the Olympics two years before in Los Angeles.

About four hours later, our team ran against Rampling's in the 4 x 440-yard relay, also called the mile relay. I was running the anchor leg, or last part of the relay, against Rampling. When I received the baton, Rampling was ahead of me by 9 yards. But I saw him ahead of me and started pounding down the cinder path. I ran all out, but I was also careful not to burn myself out too quickly as I had done in the individual race. I managed to gain about 7 yards of Rampling's lead. Still, while he beat me by a couple of yards, I managed to gain enough ground to help bring our team a second-place finish.

Later that afternoon, Lord Lonsdale presented our medals. Lord Lonsdale was a boxing aficionado and sportsman. He was famous for helping to implement the

Marquis of Queensberry Rules, a series of strict rules that ensured fair play in boxing.

I was on the podium. Lord Lonsdale put the silver medal around my neck and said to me, "Laddie, I thought for sure you were going to catch him!" and he gave me a wink.

I smiled and replied, "Your Lordship, I did my best."

After our competition, we were given tours of London and the surrounding countryside. This also included visits with royalty, and our team was presented to Great Britain's Prince Edward.

We were also given a dinner in our honor by Lord Desborough, who was well known as a high-profile sports figure and a supporter of athletics. The meal was held at the Goldsmith Company on Foster Lane in London, and our meals were presented to us on gold and silver plates. As we arrived at the dinner, a butler greeted us at the door and took the gold-embossed card we had been given as an invitation. He held the card in a white-gloved hand and announced us in a grand, rich British voice as we entered the hall.

I'll never forget my introduction: "*Mr. Raymond Lewis of Canada.*" As he said "of Canada" I felt a surge of pride. The sound of his voice rippled through the grand hall of the building. I immediately thought of my old foes, Captain Cornelius and Robert Hunter.

If only they were here to see this moment, I thought to myself.

CHAPTER 14

CROSSING THE FINISH LINE

◆

After we returned to Canada, I continued to do well in track events. I clocked 48 seconds in the quarter-mile at Toronto's Exhibition Stadium track, a great time and equal to that of Godfrey Rampling at the British Empire Games. In September of that same year, I won the Canadian championship in the 440 yards.

When I was training outdoors, I ran with the sun at my back or at my side, so that I could watch the movement of my arms and legs. This way, I could correct my running, keeping my back straight and ensuring that I didn't swing my arms too much. This is something that I taught myself and didn't learn from any coach. Indoors, I was also self-taught. I may have been an even better indoor runner than outdoor runner, as I taught myself how to run on the curves of the wooden track, pivoting on my hips and finding the right spot to move to, in order to gain an advantage over the competition.

I ran in several outdoor competitions in 1935 and into the winter season of 1936. For an indoor meet at the Forum in Montreal, the Forum's manager, Tommy

baid my expenses to travel to the meet. He sent
ollars – a lot of money at the time. I went on
to win the 600-yard run. Indoor meets could be rough
competitions and runners would often bump into each
other, sometimes swinging an elbow or driving a fist –
"accidentally" of course – into a competitor to knock him
off balance.

In that race, I passed a runner who reached and gave
me a hard knock on my arm. But it didn't stop me from
winning the race. I later found out that the runner was
Elton Brown. Brown was on Pittsburgh State University's
list of All-Time Top Performers. He was the junior
national champion of the U.S., who had also come second
to the U.S. senior national champion. So I didn't feel too
bad about beating someone of Brown's caliber.

In the spring of 1936 I began getting ready for the
Olympic trials. My training went well. I ran with other
top Canadian athletes in different cities during my work
as a porter. I also went to Milwaukee and trained with the
great American runner Ralph Metcalfe for two weeks
before the trials. But in Milwaukee I developed severe
shin splints.

Today, shin splints are known as medial tibia stress
syndrome. They affect the tendons that connect the
muscles to the bones on the front of the leg. The tendons
are stretched and often have small tears in them. Shin
splints happen as a result of excessive stress and strain
from running. And are they ever painful! Today, there are

many different ways to treat shin splints. But in my time as an athlete, there was little that you could do for this condition, except to retire from competitive running.

Only a few months shy of my twenty-sixth birthday, I knew I was finished as a top runner. Still, I was determined to go to Montreal for the Olympic trials. Despite the pain in my legs, I managed to make it to finals for the trials, but was beaten by some of Canada's best runners, coming fifth. Since they took only the top four finishers, I lost my chance to make the team. I would compete for two more years after that as I eased away from running.

I competed in the last meet of my track-and-field career in January 1938. My retirement from running was final at age twenty-seven. I looked back on my career: seventeen high-school championships outdoors; the national indoor champion at the 600 yards for five years; the 1932 Olympic bronze medal, and the silver medal at the 1934 British Empire Games. I had enough trophies and medals to fill a room.

With running behind me, I had to think about continuing to make a living. I wanted to get married, buy a house, and have kids. Times were often tough as a railway porter, and I would find different ways to earn money. Many times, I worked cleaning basements, stripping wallpaper, painting houses – anything to earn a dollar.

By the time World War II was underway, I needed money as I was preparing to get married. Despite logging thousands of lonely kilometers on the Canadian Pacific

Railway back and forth across the country, I had finally found someone with whom I wanted to spend the rest of my life. I met my wife Vivienne at a church social in Vancouver in 1940. The church social had a fashion show and, when I saw her up on the model's runway, I turned to a friend and said, "Who is that beautiful girl? I want to marry that lady." It was really love at first sight. Vivienne and I were married in 1941 and we spent our honeymoon traveling from Vancouver by train to Milwaukee for a few days, then to Chicago, and finally New York City.

Not long after the wedding, I was sent a draft notice to serve in the Canadian Army. I was told to report to Toronto's Exhibition Grounds, the site of the Canadian National Exhibition, to be examined for military fitness. It was a place I was familiar with, having competed there many times.

More than a million Canadians would serve in World War II. The treatment of black men in the military was much the same during World War II as it was in the First World War. Some were discriminated against, some weren't; there were those who were accepted and others for whom excuses were created to keep them out of the service. There is no record of how many black Canadians served in World War II, though most who did serve ended up in working in construction or service crews. At the same time, there were those who were able to cross the color barrier and serve with distinction as combat soldiers, sailors, and pilots.

The examination for military fitness took place over
two days. I arrived on a gray, overcast day and reported to
the Exhibition Grounds, lining up with my draft papers in
hand. I joined the long line of young men, some eager for
duty, others less so. A young doctor checked me out and
found me physically fit. In the evening I returned home to
Hamilton and headed back to Toronto the next day.

There, the fellow in charge, a white man, told me
they owed me money to cover my accommodations for
the night. He gave me the required seven dollars and then
looked at me and smirked. I could sense that a racist
comment would be coming from him.

"You might want to take that seven bucks and go out
and find a crap game," he said, laughing, referring to the
stereotype of black men gambling away their money. I
gave him an angry look. "Can you repeat that?" I asked,
bracing myself for a verbal fight. He hesitated and I
walked away.

In my final exam, designed to see if I was psychologi-
cally ready to go to war, the doctor asked me if I wanted
to fight against Adolph Hitler, the head of the German
government that was attacking many of the other countries
in Europe. Hitler was infamous for his hatred of Jews,
blacks, the Romani people (who were formerly called
Gypsies), and others. Hitler would put six million Jews
to death during the Holocaust.

My feeling was that there were many people like
Hitler right here in Canada – and I knew that because I
had encountered them. I told him so, and added, "I don't

know Hitler, but if they let me shoot some of the Hitlers
who are right here in Canada I'd be glad to go." The
doctor gave me a 4F ranking, which deferred me from
service on medical grounds. I was told later it was because
of having flat feet, a condition the doctor said sometimes
affected runners. But I never found out if it was really
flat feet or if they just didn't want an angry black man in
the service.

I continued working on the railway during the war, when
the railway companies became famous for transporting
soldiers back and forth across the country. The railways
were an important part of getting those soldiers from
point A to point B, and advertisements called on the
patriotism of our regular passengers to understand that
they may not have their usual accommodations because
of "our boys who serve."

Vivienne worked at the Otis Elevator Company,
which had been converted to a war plant, making ammu-
nition and parts for weapons. She was one of more
than 250,000 Canadian women who would work in
the factories that made munitions during the war.
Canadian factories like Otis produced 878 ships, 6000
tanks, 16,000 aircraft, and 800,000 military vehicles.

Vivienne began work at the plant as a cleaner, scrubbing the toilets and washing the floors. Later on, she
and another black woman kept after management to
give them a job on the shop floor. Finally, she got a job

working on the milling machines that made gun barrels. It was a real breakthrough for her and for other black workers who would find new opportunities because of the war effort.

Still, during the war, many old attitudes persisted. For instance, I knew a captain in the Canadian military who urged me to sign up. "Sign up with me, Ray, and I can get you on as my batman," he said. A batman was a personal servant who took care of the needs of a commanding officer, keeping his clothes tidy and shining his shoes.

"No thanks," I said. "If you mean I'm going to go and fight Hitler all the way over in Europe and spend my time there shining your shoes, I might as well stay safe here on the railroad and shine shoes for the passengers."

During the war, we saw Japanese-Canadians, accused of being spies for Japan, being moved inland from the coastal areas. At the same time, Canadians of German and Italian descent, also considered enemies of Canada, had also been moved. But more Japanese-Canadians than any other group were moved far from their homes, into the interior of Canada, despite the fact that the majority had been born here and their roots in this country went back many decades. Still, they were treated as prisoners. They were kept in internment camps. Their property and businesses were taken away from them. Many young Japanese-Canadian men were put to work building bridges and highways, at little or no pay. I was also shocked at seeing not just young Japanese-Canadian men being moved, but entire families – grandmothers, babies – all of them moved to camps far inland. It didn't surprise me that the government would treat its citizens this way.

The Japanese-Canadians I had met were hard-working and smart people. But the kind of fear that white people had of their fellow Canadians who looked different led to them being separated from the rest of society. It was racism at its worst. A white man I had considered a friend once said to me, "Ray, I'd rather live next to you than next to a Jap!" He smiled when he said it, as if he were paying me a compliment. I guess at the time he figured I was the lesser of two evils. I recall seeing job postings in store windows: "White help only!" In restaurants, owners were proud to announce to customers that they had "no Chinese or Japanese workers in the kitchen."

The hatred against minorities continued through the war years. In the United States, especially the southern U.S., getting from one place to another by train was difficult for blacks. In the north, blacks and whites traveled in the same cars. But around Washington, D.C., the invisible line where the mixing of black and white passengers took place was drawn. A train would come into a station and, for those passengers continuing south, the conductor would quietly ask the black passengers to "change cars" and move to a rail car that carried only black passengers. "I'm sorry, but you will have to leave this car," the conductor would say with a tip of his cap. "I'll be pleased to show you to the appropriate one."

During wartime, my brother-in-law Herman, who
had served overseas, was traveling across the country on
an assignment from the Army. He was on the train that I
was working on, going east from Vancouver. He was
seated by the steward in the dining car at the same table
as two white women, neither of whom he knew. It was the
custom that strangers were often seated together during
dinner in order to make the most of available space.

On seeing Herman, one of the women was very upset.
She promptly got up and disappeared from the car. Not
long after, the steward informed Herman that he would
have to change tables, as the woman was from the southern U.S. and complained that she wouldn't be seated at
the same table as a black man. I watched as the steward,
a good fellow on excellent terms with the porters, apolo-
gized profusely to Herman, explaining that if he had
refused the woman's demand he could have lost his job.

On another trip, Vivienne was traveling to San
Francisco to see her sister. She was washing up in the
washroom and another woman, who was white, asked
Vivienne where she lived. When Vivienne replied, the
woman lamented that she was from California. "And it's
getting so bad there because all of the black people are
moving in. It makes you want to pack up and leave the
neighborhood." The woman had mistaken Vivienne for
white because of her light skin.

"Is it so bad that they're moving in?" asked Vivienne.

"Of course! Don't you think so?" the woman replied.

"Well, I really don't know," Vivienne answered. "I mean, I'm black myself. How could I judge?" The woman's jaw dropped and she hustled out of the room.

But changes, big changes, in the economy and in the way people saw themselves, were taking place because of the war. World War II was important both in terms of world history and in our country's social history. It created job opportunities for women in industry and gave blacks, both men and women, a chance to advance into different occupations. After the war, there were more jobs as the economy grew. Universities and colleges were being built to accommodate the soldiers coming back from the war. In greater numbers, blacks were given access to a university education, and many new Canadians came from places like the Caribbean and Asia. The prosperity led to changes in the treatment of black people, who were strengthened in their resolve to push for an end to discrimination.

In Ontario, two pieces of anti-discrimination legislation would be passed in the Legislature of Premier Leslie Frost in the early 1950s. One was the Fair Employment Practices Act, a law forbidding discrimination when employers hired people for jobs. The Fair Accommodation Practices Act forbade discrimination by landlords when people were seeking to rent apartments or houses.

A few years after we were married, Vivienne and I bought a small piece of property on Highway 20, just outside Hamilton, and were planning to build a house on it. But in order to buy it, I had to go through a white friend of mine, who was also a lawyer, to put down the money for us. Up until then, we were turned away by real estate agents whose clients would not sell their homes to black people.

But we managed to get our property and our house was built. We settled down despite being the target of a petition, started by a local woman almost as soon as we moved in, to run us out of the community because of our color. But our strength came in knowing our rights. We paid our taxes. We contributed to the community. And so we had a right to live there – and that's what kept us there. We refused to be driven out by bigots. In 1945 we adopted two boys, Larry and Tony, who were half-brothers.

We settled down and soon got to know our neighbors, even the woman who had started the petition to drive us out! We were persistent, showing kindnesses to our neighbors and teaching them something about tolerance and accepting other people despite their differences. For most of our neighbors, it was the first time they had come into contact with black people. Once the woman who started the petition got to know us, her attitude began to change. Soon she was babysitting our boys and, by the time we eventually sold our property, we were close friends with this woman and her family.

But there were other reminders of our color and the role it played in society; one time a man working for an insurance company knocked at our door. He said he was a doctor, and a staff member of the London Life Insurance Company. The company had sold a policy to my wife, who had very light skin. The doctor was at the door to determine the "percentage" of "colored blood" Vivienne had.

As I mentioned earlier, race is an invention. It's a way of looking at people that is truly an illusion. The attitudes that come with it are rooted entirely in the person who is doing the labeling. For years, white society had tried to apply "scientific" methods that labeled a person according to how much black ancestry they possessed. If you had any bit of black ancestry, you were considered black and treated accordingly. Of course, we know today that blood is just blood – its color is red, no matter who you are. And while it might be type A or type O or type AB, your skin color has absolutely nothing to do with it.

Yet, here was the insurance company doctor, standing on my doorstep with a clipboard in hand, asking me "what percentage of colored blood your wife has."

"She's 100 percent Negro," I answered, using the terminology of the time.

The doctor was a little confused. "No, no, I've examined her," he answered. "She can't be 100 percent Negro. Please tell me how much colored blood she has."

I told him again, and when he was finally convinced, I asked him if this meant that the policy was going to be more expensive.

"Yes it will," he replied. He finally left, with "100 percent Negro" noted in his records. Why was insurance more expensive for black people? It was more costly because it was believed that blacks died earlier than whites, and so they were a greater risk for an insurance company to cover. Insurance was also more expensive for people in dangerous occupations, like steeplejacks (who work at restoring historic towers and buildings) and miners who might die from a cave-in. Pullman porters also had to pay higher premiums for insurance; in the 1940s, probably 90 percent of the blacks buying insurance policies were porters. Even today, some insurance companies get into trouble because they charge their black clients higher premiums.

Attitudes didn't change when my sons went to school. They, too, encountered racism. When we lived in Stoney Creek, just outside of Hamilton, my son Larry came home from school one day and asked me, "Dad, do they have some nuts from Brazil called Nigger Toes?"

"Yes, they do, son," I said. "That's a nickname for Brazil nuts."

Larry's face was downcast. "Today my teacher said something about Nigger Toes and all the kids in the class turned around and looked at me."

I went to the school and spoke with the principal, explaining to him how offensive it was for a teacher to use the word "nigger." The principal was very apologetic and brought the teacher into the office. She too was very sorry.

"I really didn't mean anything by it, Mr. Lewis," she said. I left with a promise from the principal that it would not happen again at the school. "I will see to it that teachers are aware of how offensive that word is," he said. "I will make sure that they do not use it, and that they ensure that the children don't use it either."

On another occasion my other son Tony, who was nine at the time, came home and asked if he could speak to me privately. In his room, he sat on the edge of his bed, looking at the floor, then let out a deep sigh and began. "Dad, one of the other kids at school called me a nigger."

"What did you do?" I asked. He paused, knowing that I did not condone violence.

"I punched him, Dad. I knocked him down and laid him out flat." He was very quiet as he said this, uncertain how I would react and not wanting his mother to hear.

What could I say? My son had stood up for himself. I have to admit I felt a bit proud, as it proved he had the same fire inside of him that I had when I was his age.

"You did the right thing, son," I said. "You stood your ground and you let him know that you weren't going to take that kind of talk." We shook hands and I gave him a hug.

I loved Tony for his strength and his determination in taking on the other boy's attitude. Granted, it wasn't the kind of approach his grandparents would have taken. But he didn't back away. It's sad that only a year later, Tony would die in a swimming accident in Lake Ontario. He was a bright and happy child and I often think of what he might have achieved as an adult.

CHAPTER 15

BEING MY OWN BOSS

*In 1948, I joined the Masonic Lodge, also
called the Freemasons. My interest in the Masons
had been sparked as a child, and I had seen the
Masons at their church services when I was small.
My brother Howard went into the Lodge before me
and encouraged me to join.*

Freemasonry is a society of people who are concerned
mainly with moral and spiritual values. Its members are
taught its ideas by a series of ritual dramas. These dramas
are allegories, which use symbols that are designed to
guide people in the right direction. The basic qualification for admission into (and continuing membership in)
the Masons is a belief in a Supreme Being. Membership is
open to men of any race or religion who can fulfil this
essential qualification and who are of good repute. The
Freemasons follow three great principles: Brotherly Love,
or tolerance and respect for others; Relief, which is the
practice of charity; and Truth, the striving for truth and
high moral standards.

Our lodge was one of several that were comprised almost entirely by men of African descent. These lodges were called the Prince Hall Masonry, after Prince Hall, who was born around 1748 in Bridgetown, Barbados, in the British West Indies, the son of a white Englishman and a black woman. Prince Hall was the first Master of African Lodge No. 459, the first North American lodge of black Freemasons. He was very successful in life, as a preacher, businessman and statesman. Thanks to the dedicated efforts of Prince Hall, black men and women in the U.S. and Canada have been given an opportunity to pursue the opportunities that the Masonic Lodge represents. Our lodge is the oldest Prince Hall Lodge in Canada and was created in 1852.

In 1952, I finally left the railway. Over the course of twenty-two years, the railway porters had been unionized, which meant they had better job protection, guarantees of more regular work hours, and pay increases. When I left, the salary was about $150 a month, almost double what I was making when I started. There were black porters who were in supervisory positions, and they also held other jobs in the railway, like engineers and mechanics.

I had decided to go into business for myself, and for fifteen years I ran my own custodial services company. I had nine people working for me and started off cleaning the offices of the Westinghouse factory for about a year. After that, my company cleaned the offices of the

International Harvester Company and some of the banks in downtown Hamilton. I would work through the night, supervising my staff and doing a lot of the cleaning myself. While it wasn't always a profitable venture, I enjoyed running my own firm and being my own boss.

It was also very competitive, and eventually I had to close down my business as the competition began to outbid my company.

In 1968, I went to work as a chauffeur for a politician, George Kerr, who was a Member of the Ontario Legislature. My friend Lincoln Alexander, who would later become Ontario's Lieutenant Governor, was very kind in helping me get this job, providing me with a very good reference.

I would drive George to all of his meetings and events. George served as the Member of Provincial Parliament for Burlington South for twenty-one years, and was a Cabinet Minister for ten years. He was a very generous and kind man, and treated me well during the ten years that I worked for him. George always gave me a great deal of respect and never referred to me as his chauffeur. To George, I was always a member of his staff, not just somebody driving him from place to place.

In 1978, at age sixty-eight, I began work at the Unified Family Court in Hamilton, working as a clerk. Roy McMurtry, who was Ontario's Attorney General and would later became Chief Justice of Ontario, was someone I got to know during my time working for

George, and he had recommended that I try for a job with the court system. I worked there until I was seventy-eight years old; then I finally retired, carrying with me a lifetime of memories.

After retirement, I continued my work as a Mason. In 1996, the Masons' Supreme Council honored me for my service as deputy for Canada. All told, I logged more than a quarter of a million miles working on behalf of the Masons.

I also became very busy with a lot of public speaking engagements, especially talking to children, both black and white, about my experiences as a runner and as a porter. I hold to the notion that if people live, work, and learn together, they will overcome racial stereotypes. They will see each other as they really are, and will learn to appreciate not only their differences, but also their similarities.

I kept in touch with some of my athletic colleagues of the past, and I've had a chance to meet many of today's top athletes, like Donovan Bailey and Curtis Hibbert. I've even loaned my medals and trophies to Curtis for use in exhibits about Olympic athletes.

People often ask me to compare today's athlete with the athletes of my time, much as hockey fans ask former stars to compare today's NHL with the era of the Original Six hockey teams. My response is that it is really difficult to compare. Today everything, from shoes to clothing to the track, is different. There are dietitians and masseurs, sports psychologists and high-priced coaches. Training is

different and many amateur athletes today could almost
be considered professional. And if they don't become
millionaires, many of today's athletes can still earn a good
living as coaches, trainers, teachers, television commenta-
tors, or motivational speakers. It's a long way from the
old days of running on cinder tracks, training whenever
and wherever you could, and trying to scratch out a
living while seeing your name on a list of the world's
top athletes.

CHAPTER 16

RECOGNITION

*I never went looking for recognition, but in my
hometown of Hamilton, people began to mention
my achievements as a local athlete.*

In 1992 I was inducted into the Hamilton Gallery of
Distinction at the Hamilton Convention Centre. The
Gallery is maintained by the local Chamber of Commerce,
and was created during Hamilton Homecoming celebrations in 1984.

In 1996, I was given a place on Hamilton's Sports
Wall of Fame at Copps Coliseum. Jerry Ormand, a
former sports editor at the *Hamilton Spectator*, created the
Sports Wall of Fame in 1988. There, on the wall of a long
curving hallway on the second floor of this great sports
complex, hangs a plaque. It has a photo of me from my
running days, along with a pen-and-ink sketch from my
high-school days, the caption *Rapid Ray*, and a description
of my achievements. On the wall next to my plaque is one
honoring hockey ex-player and coach Pat Quinn; close by
is one for M.M. "Bobby" Robinson, creator of the British
Empire Games.

I was pleased with my achievements. But I knew, too, that they should be preserved for future generations of African-Canadian athletes. With that in mind, I donated my trophies and medals – along with those of my brother Howard – to the Black History and Cultural Museum in 1995. The museum is located just outside of Collingwood, in Sheffield Park on the shore of Georgian Bay. It's operated by my cousin Carolynn Wilson, and is a great place to learn about the early black pioneers in the Collingwood area. Donating my medals and trophies made me feel good, as it linked me to my mother's past, since she was raised in Collingwood.

The black community in that area was largely forgotten, and the museum has done excellent work to restore the names of families and individuals whose lives and contributions would otherwise have gone unrecognized. The museum also worked hard to re-establish African-Canadian cemeteries that were deliberately destroyed by the white population in the early years of this century, in an attempt to erase local black history. I felt the Museum was a perfect setting for my medals, which are now on display in a trophy case along with photographs of me from my early days.

In 1999, I was honored with an African-Canadian Achievement Award. Toronto's *Pride News Magazine* created the award, which recognizes the contributions made by African-Canadians. Among those who have been honored are singer Salome Bey, writer Austin Clarke, and medical doctor Titus Owolabi.

But possibly my most exciting moment came in early February 2001, when I received a letter from the Governor General's Office in Ottawa, telling me I had been chosen to receive the Order of Canada. The Order of Canada recognizes those people who have made an impact on our country, and is considered Canada's greatest honor for lifetime achievement. The Governor General, who is the Queen's official representative in Canada, presents it.

I had opened the letter with interest, and when Vivienne came into the living room, I had tears streaming down my face.

"What's wrong, Ray?" she asked and put a hand on my shoulder. I was almost speechless. After a moment, I regained my composure.

"I'm getting the Order of Canada, Vivienne," I said. "We're going to Ottawa."

A week later, I received a cheque for $250 from the Canadian Government. I thought at first that this was to cover my accommodations for the trip to Ottawa, and then later found out that we were already booked into the Chateau Laurier, one of Canada's classiest hotels, situated right next to the Parliament Buildings.

I rubbed my chin and chuckled as I thought of my days as a young man when I ran by that big hotel in the shadow of the Parliament Buildings, as I trained for the Olympics during the CPR's stops in Ottawa. I had never stayed in that hotel, because blacks were banned from it in the old days. Now, as I got ready to receive

Canada's highest honor, I was going to be staying in a beautiful suite overlooking the Ottawa River.

The ceremony was held on February 28. It was an exciting time. Newspaper reporters asked questions. Photographers' flashes popped. It was almost like the days of the Olympics and the British Empire Games, when, as the country's top athletes, glory was ours to hold.

I received a long and thunderous ovation as my name was announced and I was led up to the podium to receive the honor from Governor General Adrienne Clarkson, a wonderful and gracious woman. As the Governor General presented me with my medal, she leaned forward and said to me, "This should have happened to you a long time ago." Later on, at a dinner for the Order of Canada recipients at Rideau Hall, I was asked to sit for a few minutes to visit with the Governor General at her table.

I was amazed – and I still am – that I went from railway porter to Order of Canada recipient.

On the Governor General's web site, there is even a description of my achievements:

> He is the first Canadian-born Black athlete to stand at the victory podium and receive an Olympic medal in track-and-field. Training by running alongside the CP railway tracks and occasionally in farmers' fields, he was a member of the 4 X 400-meter relay team that won a bronze medal at the 1932 Olympic Games in Los Angeles and a silver medal at the 1934

British Empire Games in London. He contin-
ues to be an inspiration to young people in the
community, reminding them that dedication
and commitment are values to be cherished.

Every time I recall receiving the Order of Canada,
I think of what it took to get to that podium in Ottawa.
Relentless drive. Energy. A willingness to sacrifice my
own comfort for the good of my athletic endeavors.
The ability to look into the face of hatred and not hate
myself or those who would hold me back from achieving
my goals.

Those are the qualities that young people, no matter
who they are or where they live, the color of their skin
or the conditions of their life, must hold to in order to
succeed, in whatever endeavor they choose to pursue. My
life was not all that uncommon, given the times in which
I grew up. I did what I could to do well, living in the
shadow of racism and running hard to achieve those
things that were too often simply handed to other people.

Today, when I stand on my balcony and look down at
the train tracks that curve like great iron snakes into the
train station near my home, I am reminded of the time I
spent on the CPR, and how that school of hard knocks
gave me the ability to deal with adversity in life and come
out a winner.

My track-and-field equipment, my shoes and spikes –
they're gone. But I still have the two shoeshine brushes
that I bought in 1930 when I became a porter. Those

brushes were the tools of my trade, but no more important, really, than the ability to deal effectively with people in any situation, using humor and strength of character. Today, I use those brushes to buff my own shoes when I get ready to go out and speak to young people about achieving their own goals. And the shine that I bring to those shoes is as bright as the sunlight that glinted and sparkled on the Canadian Pacific Railway tracks, as I ran alongside them on the prairies, so many years ago.

1910   Born in Hamilton, Ontario.

1920   Wins first medal for running.

1929   Wins four Canadian high-school championships
        in Hamilton in one day: 100 yards, 220 yards,
        440 yards, and mile relay.

1929   Wins Canadian National Championship in
        Banff, Alberta: 440 yards.

1929   Graduates from high school, having won 17
        high-school championships.

1930   Joins Canadian Pacific Railway as porter.

1932   Wins bronze medal at Los Angeles Olympics:
        4x400-meter relay.

1934   Wins silver medal at British Empire Games,
        London, England: mile relay.

1934   Wins Canadian championship: 440 yards.

1936   Develops shin splints. Fails to make Canadian
        Olympic team.

1938   Competes in final meet of track-and-field career.

1941   Marries Vivienne Jones in Vancouver, British
        Columbia.

1945   Adopts sons Anthony and Lawrence.

1952   Finishes career as railway porter; begins custodial
        services company.

1968   Starts work as driver for MPP (Burlington)
        George Kerr.

1978   Begins work at Unified Family Court in
       Hamilton.

1988   Retires from Unified Family Court.

1992   Becomes a member of Hamilton Gallery of
       Distinction at Hamilton Convention Centre.

1995   Donates medals and trophies to Collingwood's
       Black History and Cultural Museum, Sheffield
       Park.

1996   Honored on the Hamilton Sports Wall of Fame
       at Copps Coliseum.

1999   Receives African-Canadian Achievement Award
       for his contribution to Canadian sports.

2001   Becomes a Member of the Order of Canada.

INDEX